Citybus

Belfast's buses 1973–1988

Buses in Ulster Volume 5

Will Hughes

COLOURPOINT BOOKS

This book is for the girls in my life – Marnie, Kirsten and Tracey.

It is also dedicated to the memory of Evelyn, a dear friend who passed away shortly before the book went to press.

Will Hughes was born in 1954 and is a native of Belfast. Educated at the Royal Belfast Academical Institution, he graduated in 1979 from the Glasgow College of Building and Printing with a BSc in Quantity Surveying.

Travelling back and forth, by both bus and rail, between his home in south Belfast and the city centre school, awakened his interest in public transport generally. The dwindling trolleybus fleet was his first interest but following its demise in 1968 his attention was focussed on the red and cream diesel buses of Belfast Corporation Transport Department, the forerunner of Citybus.

Will is the Northern Ireland Sub-Editor of the PSV Circle and prepares monthly reports for inclusion in their news sheets. He has also been involved in the preparation of their last three fleet books covering Northern Ireland operators. His comprehensive records have provided much of the fleet information in this book and also other volumes in the series.

For many years he has been the Honorary Chairman of local bus enthusiasts group, the Irish Transport Trust.

Will now lives in Lisburn and works for a north Belfast-based Quantity Surveying practice. He is married to Marnie and has two grown-up daughters, Kirsten and Tracey.

All rights reserved. No part of this publication may be reproduced, stored in a retrieval system or transmitted in any form or by any means, electronic, mechanical, photocopying, scanning, recording or otherwise, without the prior written permission of the copyright owners and publisher of this book.

6 5 4 3 2 1

© William D Hughes
and Colourpoint Books 2005

Designed by Colourpoint Books, Newtownards
Printed by The Universities Press (Belfast) Ltd

ISBN 1 898392 99 4

Front cover: One of the last vehicles to be delivered to the Belfast Corporation Transport Department was this 1972-built Alexander-bodied Daimler Fleetline, seen here as Citybus No 2856 (EOI 4856). The location is Donegall Square West, Belfast and No 2856 is about to depart for Roughfort, Citybus' longest route. *Paul Savage*

Back cover:

Top: The Alexander-bodied Bristol RELL6G became the standard Citybus single-decker from 1976, the last survivors running their final journeys on 31 January 2004. Number 2100 was unusual in that it was fitted with a one piece windscreen. *Raymond Bell*

Bottom: The first Daimler Fleetlines took up service in Belfast in 1962. Number 2733 was one of the Potter-bodied examples and was new in 1967. It is seen here swinging into Oxford Street on a cross-town working from Glencairn. Belfast's Central Fire Station, now the site of the Laganside court complex, can be seen to the left. *Raymond Bell*

Frontispiece: When Bristol REs began to become available from National Bus Company subsidiaries in England the opportunity was taken to acquire many of this type. This former Wilts & Dorset bus is No 714, the third Eastern Coach Works-bodied Bristol RE to carry that number. *Paul Savage*

Colourpoint Books
Jubilee Business Park
21 Jubilee Road
NEWTOWNARDS
County Down
Northern Ireland
BT23 4YH
Tel: 028 9182 0505
Fax: 028 9182 1900
E-mail: info@colourpoint.co.uk
Web-site: www.colourpoint.co.uk

CONTENTS

Foreword..4
Preface and acknowledgements 5
In the beginning 7
The Citybus fleet:
    The inherited fleet 9
    Withdrawal of older vehicles...............10
Fleet renewal:
    Swan song of the double-decker.............14
    Dawn of a new era 17
    Testing times..............................22
    Enter the big cats 26
The Troubles....................................27
Troubled times – the second-hand acquisitions 29
Helping hands...................................51
Photo section:
    The inherited fleet........................53
    Early acquisitions and loans...............66
    New vehicles...............................68
    Victims 80
    Rebuilt....................................84
    The second-hand era:
        1 – The Fleetline interlude 86
        2 – The London connection (again!) 88
        3 – The Eastern Coach Works period........98
    Emergencies 114
    RE replacements (or not!)..................118
    Rail links.................................122
    Beyond Belfast 126
    Citybus people 131
Advertising vehicles............................134
Driver training vehicles 140
Service vehicles 142
Fare structure and ticket systems 145
In preservation 149
Fleet list......................................154

Foreword
by Frank Clegg, Fellow of the Chartered Institute of Logistics and Transport

This volume of the *Buses in Ulster* series comprehensively covers the activities of Citybus Limited, with particular emphasis on its bus fleet, from the transfer of the undertaking from Belfast Corporation to the Northern Ireland Transport Holding Company and encompasses the years between 1973 and 1988. The organisation was led throughout this period by the inimitable, and highly respected, Werner Heubeck CBE, Managing Director of both Ulsterbus and Citybus. Delivery of service was overseen by the late Max Hale with engineering responsibilities under the auspices of the late Tom Campbell. It is inevitable that the content of this book is heavily influenced by the effects of civil unrest and the difficult operating conditions which pertained throughout the fifteen years.

Whilst the fleet inherited by Citybus from Belfast Corporation Transport Department had amounted to 350 operational vehicles in 1973 the requirement had reduced to 297 by 1988. The more surprising statistic is that in the intervening years regrettably 500 Citybuses were totally destroyed. I cannot record this without remembering the 12 bus platform staff who made the ultimate sacrifice and the countless others who suffered both physical and mental injury in the pursuance of their duties to maintain the province's public transport system.

Will's book reviews the Citybus fleet as it changes throughout the Heubeck years. At the outset the Company was able to complete the conversion to one person operation by late 1975, despite the mixture of vehicle types prevalent and the effects of unprogrammed destruction. The policy of standardisation on the Bristol RE, which commenced in 1976, was frustrated by the forced requirement to source 'suitable' (I jest!) second-hand vehicles.

Between 1977 and 1979 significant numbers of AEC Merlins, and later Swifts, crossed the Irish Sea for further use in the province. Having joined the Belfast Corporation Transport Department in 1967, subsequently transferring to Citybus Limited at its formation and being principally responsible for service planning, construction of schedules and associated tasks, I acquired an additional remit most certainly not listed in any job description over this three year period. Every five to six weeks I led a party of bus drivers, travelling to London on a Friday evening by Ulsterbus Express, to collect from London Transport and London Country batches of the said vehicles. The journey back on Sunday and Monday proved on each occasion to be an interesting and varied experience. The vehicles were notorious for overheating and susceptible to fuel starvation and associated problems, rarely resulting in more than two-thirds completing the journey to Belfast uninterrupted. On a number of occasions this outcome was actually less than the number of buses destroyed over the same weekend and you will find within the book an example of an ex-London Country AEC Merlin which was pressed into immediate service, having merely been driven in to Short Strand depot for fuelling and the application of a *Citylink* logo. Removal of the original owner's name, destination blind, etc were luxuries which necessity did not permit! Eventually, after subsequent purchases of used Daimler Fleetline single-deckers from other sources, at least some level of standardisation returned with recycled Bristol REs, albeit with a variety of body styles.

Having had the privilege of experiencing at first hand the uniqueness of the period, when on occasions timetables, routes and drivers duty patterns had to literally be changed overnight due to constraints in vehicle numbers or freedom of movement, reading this volume of *Buses in Ulster* has evoked so many memories for me, and I hope it will do so for you as you explore the contents.

Frank Clegg
Belfast
March 2005

Preface and acknowledgements

When Colourpoint's Norman Johnston approached me back in 2003 enquiring if I would be willing to compile Volume 5 in the *Buses in Ulster* series, I was only too happy to accept, but little did I know how much work would be involved. My interest in the bus fleets of Northern Ireland centres mainly around the vehicles and it was only when I sat down to compile the fleet lists that I realised what a task lay in front of me. Compiling those lists was the easy bit!

Belfast during the 1970s and 1980s was an interesting place for bus enthusiasts but what was to become known as 'the Troubles' could, and did, make life in general difficult and indeed dangerous. Even a brief look at the aforementioned fleet lists will give the reader some indication of the number of vehicles which were destroyed during the period covered. In addition, many other vehicles suffered various degrees of damage, and street disturbances, coupled with bomb alerts and attacks, caused serious disruption to services. Many staff suffered injury, often serious, in the course of their duties and sadly a number also lost their lives. This really brings into perspective the immense difficulty the company and its staff must have faced on occasions trying to provide any sort of public transport service to the citizens of Belfast. And still, when enthusiasts such as myself called in at the various depots we were always given a warm welcome by the staff and I must record my thanks to all those people for their time and co-operation.

One effect of the 'Troubles' was the almost constant need for replacement buses and that need saw AEC Merlins and Swifts come from London Transport, further AEC Merlins from London Country Bus Services, Daimler Fleetlines from both Potteries Motor Traction of Stoke-on-Trent and Northern General Transport of Gateshead and many Bristol RE type buses from various National Bus Company fleets. Fortunately local enthusiasts, particularly the members of the Irish Transport Trust, recorded many of these vehicles on film. I would particularly like to mention Raymond Bell, Ian Houston, Irvine Millar, Billy Montgomery, Richard Newman, Mark O'Neill, Paul Rafferty, Paul Savage and Richard Whitford who permitted me to raid their precious collections in search of suitable material to properly illustrate the book. In addition I have used a number of photographs acquired from various sources over the years; where the name of the photographer is not known, the photograph is attributed to the author's collection.

Particular thanks are also extended to Translink's John Montgomery, who in his role as Fleet Control Officer has allowed me access to official fleet records and also answered many queries relating to the fleet.

I am also indebted to Howard Cunningham who compiled the chapter on 'Citybus People' and to Irvine Millar for the chapter on 'Fare Structure and Ticket Systems'. Both were also invaluable in providing much useful historical data and checking the text where necessary. My thanks, too, to Frank Clegg for taking time out from his hectic schedule to write the foreword.

This book has taken much longer to compile than either Norman or I had anticipated but I hope you think it has been worth the wait. Many thanks to the admin staff at Colourpoint for their patience in dealing with the numerous enquires from you, the public, and also to the design team for producing such a good work. Particular thanks to Norman for his patience, support and encouragement.

One person who deserves a special word of thanks is Paul Savage who is not only a friend of many years standing but who also took over the role of Colourpoint's Transport Editor during the compilation of this book. Paul has given freely of his time both in a professional and private capacity to ensure this project was completed. His advice and assistance is greatly appreciated.

Finally I must acknowledge the patience of my wife Marnie who for several years now has been tripping over files containing notes and photographs for the book. At times she must have thought she would never see our dining table again. I'm sure she will be glad to see the book finished so that I can now get on with all those little jobs around the house and garden that await me.

Will Hughes
Lisburn
March 2005

Above: Between 1952 and 1954 Belfast Corporation Transport took delivery of 98 Harkness-bodied Daimler CVG6s and two Daimler CVD6s, numbered 350–449. Fifty-two of these passed into the Citybus operational fleet and 11 which had previously been withdrawn by the Corporation were also taken into stock and stripped for spares, before being disposed of quite quickly. The eleven were not re-numbered into the 2xxx series. Number 401, which had been withdrawn in 1972, was one of the 11. It is seen here crossing the Queen's Bridge on an inbound working from Braniel in July 1965.

Richard Newman

Opposite: On the weekend prior to the takeover all serviceable vehicles were renumbered into the 2xxx series by simply painting a '2' in front of the existing fleet number, using a stencil. Guy Arab No 346 would have been so treated, becoming No 2346 in the process. The painted fleet number can just be seen in this picture taken at Gilnahirk in 1973.

WH Montgomery

In the beginning

It was back in September 1972 that the then Secretary of State for Northern Ireland, William Whitelaw, approved plans for the merger of Belfast Corporation Transport Department and Ulsterbus Ltd. Under these proposals all vehicles, depots, staff and services operated by the Corporation were to pass to the Northern Ireland Transport Holding Company, the parent company of Ulsterbus Ltd, on 1 April 1973. Both operators would share a common management structure, the former BCT operation being renamed Citybus. In the event the NITHC did not take control until 2 April 1973.

The most noticeable change, initially, was that over the weekend prior to the takeover all serviceable vehicles were renumbered by the simple addition of 2000 to their former fleet numbers. This was to avoid duplication with the fleet numbers of certain Ulsterbus vehicles. The renumbering was carried out using stencils to add a '2' to the existing fleet number and often led to a rather crude result with differing sized fleet numbers. Over the following year, as vehicles underwent their annual test and partial or full repaint, new fleet numbers, and in some cases Ulsterbus style depot codes, were applied to the front and rear of vehicles. The Belfast Corporation coat of arms was also removed from the side panels of all vehicles at this time together with side fleet numbers, a feature used by BCT but not by Ulsterbus. In addition the legal address on the nearside of vehicles was changed to reflect the new ownership.

It had originally been intended to set up a limited company when the BCT operations were taken over in April 1973 but because of legal complications this was not finally achieved until April 1975 when Citybus Limited finally came into existence.

The Citybus fleet

The inherited fleet

Changing social trends and the increase in private car ownership, coupled with problems associated with the outbreak of the Troubles in 1969, had seen a considerable reduction in the overall size of the BCT fleet in its latter years of operation. Normal withdrawals of the Guy Arab III/Harkness and Daimler CVG6/Harkness open platform double-deckers had already commenced before the takeover but despite this approximately 20% of the inherited fleet was comprised of half cab double-deckers with open rear platforms.

The following is a summary of the official operational fleet acquired:

Chassis	Body	New	Quantity
Guy Arab III	Harkness	1950/51	24
Daimler CVG6	Harkness	1952–54	52
Leyland Atlantean	Alexander (Falkirk)	1960	1
Daimler Fleetline d/d	MH Coachworks	1962–64	124
Leyland Atlantean	MH Coachworks	1964/65	3
Daimler Fleetline d/d	Potter	1967	26
Daimler Roadliner	Potter	1968/69	17
AEC Swift	Potter	1968/69	18
Daimler Fleetline s/d	Alexander (B)	1969/70	27
Daimler Fleetline d/d	Alexander (B)	1970–73	58
		Total	350

In addition, a further three Guy Arabs and 11 Daimler CVG6s were taken over as withdrawn vehicles and, after stripping for spare parts, were quickly disposed of for scrap. Perhaps the most unusual vehicles taken over were the chassis of 12 Daimler Fleetlines (11 double-deck and one single-deck), all of which had their original bodies destroyed in street disturbances in Belfast. Following overhaul, the chassis were despatched to Alexander's (Belfast) where they were fitted with replacement bodies, being returned to service during 1973 and 1974.

A batch of twenty 33'0" long Daimler Fleetlines were in the course of delivery at the time of the takeover and five of the batch were still outstanding on the takeover date. These were subsequently delivered to their new masters, thus becoming the first new additions to the Citybus fleet.

Opposite top: The most numerous type in the Corporation fleet was the MH Coachworks-bodied Daimler Fleetline. These were built between 1962 and 1964. In Great Victoria Street in July 1965 No 672 is pursued by No 590. They have just passed the Crown public house, which is now owned by the National Trust. Both have the original style flat front which was later modified (see Nos 2600/5 on pages 56 and 57). *Richard Newman*

Opposite bottom: Belfast Corporation Transport Department Daimler Roadliner No 754 poses outside the Potter factory at Dunmore, Antrim Road, Belfast prior to delivery. These Roadliners were probably the least successful buses purchased by the Corporation and were disposed of quite quickly by Citybus. Surprisingly, this vehicle ended up on the Isle of Man where it was used as a mobile church. (see page 126). *Mark O'Neill collection*

Withdrawal of older vehicles

Ulsterbus had converted its entire fleet to one man operation by 1973 and one of the first priorities of the new Citybus management team, led by the charismatic Werner Heubeck, with Max Hale as Area Manager and Tom Campbell as Chief Engineer, was to introduce full one man operation as quickly as possible. Additionally, the half cab vehicles still on the fleet list, and obviously requiring the employment of both a driver and conductor, were all over 20 years old and overdue replacement.

At the formation of Citybus there were 74 half cab double-deckers still active, forming about 20% of the fleet. The 74 consisted of 22 Guy Arab IIIs, dating from 1950/1 and 52 Daimler CVG6s, dating from 1952–54, all with Harkness bodywork. 1973 saw a total of 24 Daimler CVGs withdrawn, seven of which had been maliciously destroyed. A further nine of the type were taken out of service in 1974 along with three Guys. All of the latter had been maliciously destroyed, along with four of the Daimler CVG6s. Included among the CVGs was No 2448 (OZ 6702), the survivor of the two tin fronted vehicles. February 1975 saw two more Guy Arabs withdrawn with the remaining 17 examples being withdrawn en-masse on 27 April. Fortunately No 2346 (MZ 7444) survives in preservation.

Fifteen of the remaining Daimler CVG6s were withdrawn between January and August 1975, including two with accident damage. Of the remaining four vehicles, Nos 2435/6 (OZ 6689/90) were retired in September with Nos 2389 (OZ 6643) and 2446 (OZ 6700) bringing down the curtain on half cab operation the following month. Two of the type, Nos 2432 (OZ 6686) and 2446, survive in preservation.

The sole survivor of the three prototype vehicles purchased by Belfast Corporation Transport Dept between 1958 and 1961, Alexander-bodied Leyland Atlantean No 2551 (5540 XI), finally succumbed in November 1975 following a major mechanical failure. This vehicle had proved troublesome all its life and spent long periods out of use. Although suitable for conversion to a one-man operated vehicle, this was the only front entrance vehicle never to be so equipped. It was sold to the Londonderry and Lough Swilly Railway Co who, despite its title, was a bus operator. Fitted with a replacement engine, it was to ply the roads of Co Donegal for another few years before being finally withdrawn and scrapped.

Most bus operators tend to work on getting a service life of 12–15 years out of their vehicles. As noted above, both the Guy Arabs and the Daimler CVG6s had far exceeded this, a number of the Guys being almost 25 years old when they were withdrawn. The outbreak of the Troubles in 1969 made it virtually impossible for first Belfast Corporation Transport Dept and then Citybus to operate any sort of normal fleet replacement programme. Whilst where possible older vehicles operated the more vulnerable routes, it was not always possible to prevent newer vehicles falling victim to rioters. Consequently older vehicles that should have been withdrawn had to be maintained in service to plug gaps in the fleet.

Twenty-seven of the 151 MH Coachworks-bodied Daimler Fleetlines built for Belfast Corporation Transport Dept between 1962 and 1964 had already been destroyed prior to the formation of Citybus and of the 124 survivors, a further 102 of the type were to fall victim of the Troubles between 1973 and 1980. The first 'normal' withdrawal of the type took place in October 1978 when No 2566 (566 EZ) was taken out of service. The remaining 21 vehicles were withdrawn between April 1979 and March 1981 when the last survivor, No 2600 (600 EZ) was withdrawn. Both this and similar vehicle No 2596 (596 EZ) survived for a short time in preservation. The security ramps outside police stations and other security installations had caused serious damage to both the chassis and body outriggers of these vehicles. Many of those that survived the Troubles were withdrawn following serious chassis or body failures. Such was the condition of the chassis on the two preserved examples that both were eventually scrapped.

The three somewhat unloved MH Coachworks-bodied Leyland Atlanteans remained in service until 1977, although frequently spending long periods out of service defective. When Ulsterbus were looking for

On withdrawal Daimler Fleetline No 2596 passed to the Irish Transport Trust for preservation but the chassis was in such poor condition that it, unfortunately, had to be scrapped. Before that No 2596 was used for a couple of years to promote the Sealink shipping service between Larne in Co Antrim and the Scottish port of Stranraer and is known to have journeyed to Stranraer on at least one occasion, probably the only MH Coachworks-bodied Fleetline ever to have done so.
Paul Savage

a number of double-deckers to replace ageing Leyland Titan PD3s on heavily loaded school workings, the opportunity was taken to cascade these vehicles to Ulsterbus for operation in the northwest of the province. They fared little better with their new masters, No 2704 (1704 MZ) lasting a mere nine months, No 2705 (1705 MZ) little over a year and No 2706 (1706 MZ) just over 18 months. None of the trio survived long enough to receive Ulsterbus livery.

Of the 26 Potters-bodied Daimler Fleetlines taken into the Citybus fleet, ten were maliciously destroyed between 1974 and 1979. Number 2713 (713 UZ) was withdrawn in February 1977 following an accident and between June 1977 and April 1978, fourteen of the survivors were transferred to Ulsterbus for use on schools services in the Coleraine and Londonderry areas, the last example surviving on these duties until 1982. The one remaining vehicle, No 2733 (733 UZ) was not transferred to Ulsterbus on account of its nonstandard gearchange. It was, however, loaned to them in November 1981 but was returned the following March following accident damage and was subsequently withdrawn. Included in the transfer was the sole surviving Alexander (Belfast)-bodied rebody No 2716 (716 UZ). This vehicle became the first open topper in the Ulsterbus fleet in 1981, a role it was to fulfil for a further 12 years. Number 2712 (712 UZ) returned to the Citybus fleet in April 1982 as a driver training vehicle, being finally withdrawn in 1983.

In this September 1975 view, Daimler Roadliner 2754 is seen resting at Short Strand depot having just been driven off the steam wash, where it has been replaced by Fleetline double-decker No 2805.
Raymond Bell

The seventeen Potters-bodied Daimler Roadliners taken into the fleet were all destined to have relatively short lives with Citybus. The high revving Cummins engine and the rubber bushes used in the suspension were to be the achilles heel of the type. Many mainland operators dispensed with these troublesome vehicles at the first available opportunity. Had it not been for the heavy toll the Troubles were inflicting on the fleet, Citybus would probably have withdrawn them a lot earlier. One was withdrawn in 1973 after being hijacked and destroyed, the first 'normal' withdrawal taking place the following year after a major failure. A further two were withdrawn in 1975, with five more going in 1976, one having been maliciously destroyed. A further two were to be destroyed in 1977, the remaining six being withdrawn the same year. In a rather bizarre twist, one, No 754, was resold for use as a mobile church on the Isle of Man (see page 126). It eventually returned to Northern Ireland, operating for a short time in the Co Armagh area.

The eighteen Potters-bodied AEC Swifts fared a little better although this model was not without its problems. When built Nos 2760/3/5/8/70/1 (760/3/5/8/70/1 UZ) had been fitted with plastic body panels as an experiment to see if it would reduce the need for annual repainting. These panels had a tendency to ripple in warm weather giving these vehicles a most unusual appearance. In addition to their mechanical shortcomings there were also serious structural weaknesses in the body. One was withdrawn in 1974 after being maliciously destroyed, four more meeting the same fate in 1977. A further example was destroyed in 1978, the year the first 'normal' withdrawals took place when six were taken off the road. The remaining six vehicles were withdrawn in 1979. Major mechanical or body failures were responsible for many of these withdrawals, a number having literally shaken themselves to pieces.

After their somewhat unhappy experience with the Daimler Roadliner and AEC Swift, Belfast Corporation Transport Dept reverted to the tried and tested Daimler Fleetline for its next purchases, albeit in single-deck form. Whilst mechanically reliable, this batch of vehicles was not without its problems. Both the Daimler Roadliner and the AEC Swift had rear, horizontal, underfloor mounted engines which gave the chassis a better overall weight distribution. The Daimler Fleetline however had a vertically mounted engine situated at the extreme rear of the chassis. This tended to cause flexing of the chassis and coupled with the introduction of a centre exit at probably the weakest point in the chassis, caused major structural problems in the bodies especially around the centre exit doors. The decision to convert the surviving vehicles to standee layout in 1975/6 probably exacerbated the problem and towards the end of their lives many of these vehicles displayed quite visible cracks in the internal body and roof linings close to the centre exit. This batch of vehicles suffered particularly badly during the Troubles. Of the 27 taken into the Citybus fleet, 24 were to be destroyed between 1974 and 1981. Number 2783 (AOI 783) was withdrawn and scrapped in July 1979 following accident damage. The two surviving vehicles, Nos 2785/6 (AOI 785/6) were withdrawn and scrapped in 1982.

Of the 65 dual-door double-deck Daimler Fleetlines delivered to Belfast Corporation Transport Dept prior to the takeover, only 58 remained. Seven had been destroyed as a result of the Troubles, two of which were awaiting rebody. Between 1974 and 1987 a further 34 of the type were to fall victim to the Troubles, two of which were subsequently rebodied. The first 'normal' withdrawal took place in October 1981 when No 2842 (AOI 842) was taken out of service and scrapped. In May 1983 a further three – Nos 2825/48/9 (AOI 825/48/9) – were taken out of traffic. Of these Nos 2825/49 became driver training vehicles, the other example being scrapped. The end of the school term in June 1983 saw the withdrawal of the 13 remaining examples from the initial batch of 50 – Nos 2803/19/30/2/5/9/44–7/50–2. Of these No 2819 (AOI 819) was scrapped but the remaining 12 vehicles were held in secure storage. This left only Nos 2854/5/6/8/9/61/2/6/9 (EOI 4854/5/6/8/6/61/2/6/9) from the second batch in service. Heavy steering had always been a problem with these vehicles resulting in numerous complaints from drivers. In an effort to cure this problem and prolong the lives of these vehicles, the decision was taken to fit the survivors with power steering. Citybus was also keen to rid themselves of the survivors of the newer, but troublesome, batch of Leyland Atlanteans, Nos 2873–2912 (JOI 2873–2912). As a result it was decided to also overhaul and reinstate the 12 previously stored examples, fitting them with power steering at the same time. All returned to service in 1984/5 but No 2835 (AOI 835) did not survive long, being withdrawn in May 1985. Number 2856 (EOI 4856) was withdrawn in 1986 with No 2852 (AOI 852) going the following year. Final withdrawal for the bulk of the survivors came in 1988 when Nos 2803/30/2/9/44–7/50/1 (AOI 803/30/2/9/44–7/50/1) and 2854/61/6/9 (EOI 4854/61/6/9) were taken out of service. Of these Nos 2846/51 (AOI 846/51) had suffered accident damage. The two remaining vehicles, Nos 2858/62 (EOI 4858/62), were finally withdrawn in January 1989 bringing to an end the operation of double-deck vehicles in everyday service in Belfast.

The last of the Alexander-bodied Daimler Fleetline single-deckers to remain in service were Nos 2785/6. Both were withdrawn in 1982 and No 2785 is seen here at Ormeau. This was an unusual working, No 2785 being Falls-based, and had occurred as a result of disturbances the previous evening. Interestingly, this turning circle can no longer be used and the background has completely changed, disappearing under another retail development. *Paul Savage*

Fleet renewal

Swan song of the double-decker

The first new vehicles to be received by Citybus were the five outstanding 33'0" long Daimler Fleetline double-deckers – Nos 2863/5/70–2 (EOI 4863/5/70–2) – from the final batch of 20 ordered by Belfast Corporation. Of these No 2863 lasted less than seven weeks before being hijacked and destroyed in an incident which sadly also cost a passenger their life. This, however, was not to be the end for No 2863. The virtually undamaged chassis was overhauled and returned to Alexander's where it received a replacement body, returning to service in May 1974. Ironically this vehicle was to go on to be the longest survivor of the type. Following a spell as a driver training vehicle in 1988/89, it was converted to open-top layout in 1991 and continued to perform this role until withdrawn and sold for scrap in 2002.

Following delivery of the five outstanding Daimler Fleetlines, attention was turned to building replacement bodies on the 11 double-deck and one single-deck chassis taken over from Belfast Corporation Transport Department. Nine of the double-deck chassis were 30'0" long Daimler Fleetlines which had previously carried MH Coachworks or Potters bodies. The new Alexander (Belfast) bodies closely followed the original MH Coachworks design and the end result was a most attractive vehicle. One major difference was that the bodies were constructed on aluminium frames; the original bodies were on steel frames. They also had rubber mounted glazing unlike the original vehicles where the windows were mounted in aluminium window pans. Delivery of the nine vehicles took place between September 1973 and February 1974. Sadly most of them only had short lives, one being destroyed in 1975 and seven more meeting the same fate in 1977. The sole survivor, 2716, was eventually transferred to Ulsterbus in 1981 and after a period on school bus duties in Coleraine, was converted to an open-topper in July 1981. It was to continue in this role until August 1993 when it was replaced by a newer vehicle.

The remaining two double-deck rebodies were on the 33'0" long Daimler Fleetline chassis. With these vehicles the bodies were identical to the original Alexander (Belfast) dual-door bodies except that they had aluminium framing as opposed to the original steel. Delivered in June 1973 and March 1974, both lasted until 1979 when they were destroyed for a second time.

The final rebody did not enter service until November 1974 and this was the 36'0" long single-deck Daimler Fleetline chassis. When originally built No 2774 had a 43-seat dual-door body with space for 15 standing passengers. However when it returned to service following rebodying it had only 32 seats with space for 47 standees, giving it roughly the same total capacity as a double-decker. Standee buses, whilst popular on mainland Europe, had never enjoyed the same support with United Kingdom operators. Little did we know at the time but this vehicle was to set the benchmark for future single-deck deliveries to the Citybus fleet.

One of the first priorities of Citybus management was to replace the remaining, and by now life expired, half-cab double-deckers and to this end an order was quickly placed for 80 (later reduced to 40) Leyland Atlantean AN68/2R with Alexander (Belfast) 86-seat bodies (Nos 2873–912, JOI 2873–912). The choice of chassis more reflected Ulsterbus thinking rather than that of the former BCT engineering staff who had favoured the Gardner-engined Daimler Fleetline. Four Leyland Atlantean PDR1/1 vehicles had been purchased by the Corporation Transport Department – one in 1960 and three in 1964/5 – but these vehicles had never proved either popular or reliable and had spent long periods off the road.

Whilst sharing the model name, the AN68 chassis had little in common with the earlier PDR type. The body was very similar to that fitted to Daimler Fleetlines Nos 2803–72, albeit with only a front entrance/exit in place of the dual entrance/exit of the Fleetlines and the staircase was once again moved to the offside of the vehicle from the nearside. Unlike the dual-door Daimler Fleetlines which had steel framed bodies, these vehicles were the first in the fleet to have aluminium framed bodies, a feature which was to ultimately lead to their premature demise. Other Ulsterbus features to appear on these vehicles were the use of galvanised steel front and rear bumpers and side rubbing strips.

Delivery of these vehicles took place between August 1975 and March 1976, with all 40 being allocated to Ardoyne depot. They were destined never to see service as a complete batch, as No 2908 was hijacked and destroyed in February 1976 after only three weeks in service. Two more, Nos 2890 and 2909, were to meet a similar fate in September 1976; consideration was given to rebodying these three vehicles. With the switch away from double-deck vehicles these plans were ultimately abandoned and the chassis were dismantled for spare parts.

Speed ramps to slow down vehicles outside police stations and other security installations were commonplace at this time and these caused considerable damage to both the chassis and bodies of these vehicles. Flexing of the chassis as the vehicle negotiated these ramps led to failures in the chassis outriggers. The aluminium framing did not have the rigidity of the steel framing and led to serious structural failures in the body, especially around the rear wheel arches and in the floor structure, resulting in expensive repairs being necessary. The generally poor condition of the Antrim Road on which many of these vehicles operated

It came as a bit of a surprise when the first new vehicles ordered for Citybus were 40 Leyland Atlantean AN68s, given the Corporation's allegiance to the Gardner-engined Daimler Fleetline. The Atlanteans were generally popular with drivers but the Alexander bodies gave great trouble, mainly as a reult of speed ramps outside police stations and security forces bases and also the poor condition of the Antrim Road. Number 2891 is pictured here sitting on the square setts at Cregagh terminus, in southeast Belfast, and is about to set off across the city to Glencairn in the north.

Paul Savage

only added to the problems. As with the earlier inherited Atlanteans they were not considered to be a success and all had relatively short lives.

Ardoyne depot was at this time a popular target for terrorist attacks and no fewer than 14 of the Atlanteans were destroyed in fire bomb attacks on the depot between April 1978 and July 1980. A further example of the type was destroyed in a similar attack on Falls Park depot in January 1989 and nine of the type were hijacked and destroyed whilst out on service. Normal withdrawal of the 16 survivors commenced in June 1983 and all were gone by November 1984, after a service life of only seven to eight years. Number 2893 subsequently passed to Ulsterbus Ltd where it was converted to an open-topper, entering service at Coleraine depot in April 1986. It was finally withdrawn in March 1995 and was then stored for over eight years before being finally scrapped. Two also survived for a period as playbuses with the Voluntary Services Bureau in Belfast.

A further two double-deckers, Nos 2829 and 2857, were delivered in 1976 when additional 33'0" long Daimler Fleetline chassis were overhauled and dispatched to Alexander (Belfast) to be rebodied. Both had been destroyed in 1974 and on their return to service in April 1976, they were fitted with H49/37F bodies, similar to those fitted to the Leyland Atlanteans, in place of the H46/31D bodies originally carried. Number 2829 was destroyed once more in January 1979 in a firebomb attack on Falls Park depot. This vehicle was unique in the BCT/Citybus fleet in that it was the only vehicle in the fleet to be rebodied twice and destroyed three times!

In 1994 Daimler Fleetline No 2857 was disposed of as scrap following a major mechanical failure. However it was recovered and underwent a major restoration at Falls Park workshops, later being being presented to the Ulster Folk and Transport Museum at Cultra, Holywood, Co Down. It is seen here immediately after the presentation ceremony in company with Raymond Bell's Belfast Corporation Guy Arab III/Harkness No 346, which, incidentally, had also served with Citybus as its No 2346 (see also pages 7 and 149). Number 2857 has been dedicated to the memory of the Citybus and Ulsterbus staff who lost their lives during the Troubles. *Paul Savage*

Number 2857 remained in service until March 1994 when it was withdrawn following an engine failure. It was dispatched to Beattie, Hillsborough for scrapping but had a lucky escape when a change of heart saw it retrieved and taken to Falls Park workshops for a thorough overhaul. Also retrieved at the same time was former Citybus No 2716 (716 UZ) which had latterly been used by Ulsterbus as an open-topper. It was to donate its running units to No 2857 before it was once again returned to the scrap yard and broken up. Following overhaul No 2857 was presented to the Ulster Folk and Transport Museum at Cultra, Co Down and is currently on display in the transport gallery, along with restored Belfast Corporation Transport Department Guy BTX trolleybus No 112. Number 2857 has been dedicated to the memory of the Citybus and Ulsterbus staff who lost their lives during the Troubles.

In the event Nos 2829/57 turned out to be the last new double-deck vehicles to be delivered to either fleet and it would be some 25 years before new double-deckers would again be seen on the streets of Belfast.

Dawn of a new era

Back in 1967 Ulsterbus had carried out a series of comparative trials between a Marshall-bodied AEC Swift and an Eastern Coach Works-bodied Bristol RE to determine the most suitable vehicle for future orders for city and urban type vehicles. Following on from the trials an order was placed for 20 Bristol RELL6Ls, with bodies to be built by Potters, Belfast, for use on Londonderry city services. Right from the beginning Ulsterbus were enthusiastic supporters of local industry and were keen, where possible, that the body orders were placed with local coachbuilders. In the event Potters were unable to complete the order in the specified timescale and the order was transferred to the Alexander plant at Falkirk. Delivered in 1969, these were to be the first of 620 similar vehicles to be purchased by Ulsterbus and later Citybus. Ironically by the time these vehicles had been delivered, Potters had been taken over by Alexander's and the Alexander (Belfast) plant had come into being.

It might seem odd to include a picture of an Ulsterbus Bristol RE in a book on Citybus but the success of the 20 vehicles delivered in 1968 for use on Londonderry City Services was such that they helped determine the vehicle purchasing policy for many years thereafter. Of that initial 20 only one, No 1058, survives and it is seen here at Foyle Street, Derry on a damp day in 1984. It was at one time jointly owned by the author.

Paul Savage

By the time it came to placing orders for further vehicles, the Bristol RE had been dropped from the model range, at least for the domestic market. Bristol was by this time part of the Leyland Motors empire and it ultimately decided to rationalise its model range. As a result the AEC Swift, Bristol RE, Daimler Roadliner and Fleetline (single-decker) and the Leyland Panther and Panther Cub were dropped, to be replaced by the all-encompassing Leyland National. This was to be a fully integral vehicle built at a new production facility at Workington, Cumbria. Of the models dropped only the Bristol RE could have been described as a success; the rest all had their failings and, indeed, some were outright disasters.

Leyland Motors attempted to persuade Ulsterbus to standardise on the Leyland National and to this end supplied them with a demonstrator in October 1972. It was allocated fleet number 3 and was registered EOI 8060. After four months on demonstration duties it was purchased by Ulsterbus as their fleet number 1600 and was allocated to Londonderry, for use on the city services, where it worked alongside the original batch of Bristol REs. The Leyland 510 engine fitted to this vehicle proved to be the achilles heel of the type. The National was also fitted with numerous trip switches and interlocks which were constantly causing the vehicle to cut out whilst in service, something which obviously did not endear it to the passengers, drivers or engineers! In short, it was simply too complicated when compared to what Ulsterbus was used to, although when compared to today's modern low floor vehicles, even the Leyland National seems prehistoric. Being a one-off vehicle it also spent long periods out of service awaiting spare parts. In addition, as it was of integral construction, there was no possibility of there being any local input in the construction of the bodies.

In an effort to force Leyland Motors hand, Ulsterbus hinted that they were talking to a number of foreign manufacturers with a view to finding a suitable chassis to meet their requirements. Although denied to domestic customers, the Bristol RE was still available as an export chassis with large numbers being exported to New Zealand. When it became apparent that Ulsterbus would not buy the Leyland National, Leyland conveniently reclassified Northern Ireland as an export market and an initial order was placed for forty vehicles.

Although by this time Citybus had come into being, all of the initial order was allocated to the Ulsterbus fleet. Unlike the earlier Leyland-engined vehicles, these vehicles were fitted with the Gardner 6HLX engine, a make of engine more associated with the former Belfast Corporation Transport Department fleet rather than that of Ulsterbus. The body order was placed with Alexander (Belfast) for 28 with 44-seat dual-door bodies, for service in Lurgan, Portadown and on Londonderry city services, the remaining 12 vehicles to have 50-seat single entrance bodies, for use at Oxford Street and Bangor depots.

The body style closely followed that used for the original batch although there were a number of minor styling changes. A major problem at this time was vandalism and in particular broken windows. To this end these vehicles were fitted with forced air ventilation and fixed plain glazing, a feature that was to become standard on all future deliveries to both fleets. The engines on the dual-door vehicles were rated at 140 bhp whilst those on the single-door vehicles were rated at 150 bhp, both coupled to a five speed gearbox. All were delivered during 1975, the dual-door vehicles being numbered 2001–28 (JOI 3001–28) and the single-door vehicles 2029–40 (JOI 3029–40). Single entrance vehicles from later batches of the type quickly replaced the dual-door vehicles based at Lurgan and Portadown and the dual-door vehicles were transferred to Londonderry to join their sisters on the city services.

A follow up order was placed for a further 130 vehicles of this type, this time fitted with the Gardner 6HLXB engine coupled to a four speed semi automatic gearbox. All of this order were to be fitted with dual-door bodies and only 15 vehicles from the batch were allocated to the Ulsterbus fleet. Allocated fleet numbers 2121–35 and registered MOI 2121–35, they entered service in 1976/7 at the former Smithfield depot.

The remaining 115 vehicles were allocated to the Citybus fleet and were delivered in three batches during 1976/7 – Nos 2041–80 (LOI 2041–80), Nos 2081–120 (MOI 8081–120) and Nos 2136–70

(POI 2136–70). Unlike the Ulsterbus vehicles, which had seats for 44, all of the Citybus vehicles had only 32 seats with space for 47 standees. Following the rebodying of single-deck Daimler Fleetline No 2774 (AOI 774) in November 1974, the decision was taken that the bulk of future deliveries for the Citybus fleet would be to this layout. In March 1975 Potters-bodied AEC Swift No 2756 (756 UZ) was rebuilt from B46F to B30F with space for 37 standees. However the PSV authorities were not happy with the standee layout in this type of vehicle and it was returned to its original seating configuration without ever entering service. Between December 1975 and May 1976, the 24 surviving single-deck Alexander-bodied Daimler Fleetlines were reseated from B43D to B31D with space for 47 standees. No consideration was given to converting the dual-door Potters-bodied Daimler Roadliners to standee layout as it had already been decided that these troublesome vehicles would be eliminated from the fleet at the earliest opportunity and, indeed, several had already been withdrawn.

The first appearance of the new Bristol RE was at the Lord Mayor's Show on 22 May 1976 when No 2054 (LOI 2054) took part. The vehicle carried a new livery of mainly ivory with a red waistband and a broad red band at the skirt, applied in the same layout as the Ulsterbus livery.

The new Bristol REs proved to be both popular with both drivers and engineering staff but the same could not be said for the travelling public. The standee layout wasn't at all popular and passengers' misery was further compounded by the fact that in an effort to reduce vandalism, all seat backs and seat squabs were solid glass fibre. (This was later changed to just the rear four rows.) Not only were these seats uncomfortable, it also proved very difficult to remain on them when vehicles were cornering at speed and manys a passenger found themselves dumped in a heap in the aisle!

The first Bristol REs for Citybus arrived in 1976 and, unlike the 20 in Londonderry, were Gardner-engined. Falls allocated No 2053 is pictured here in Wellington Place en route to its depature point in Castle Street. Note that at this time the street lighting was still carried on the redundant trolleybus poles. *Author*

Apart from the 15 vehicles delivered in 1979 for use on private hire duties the first Citybus Bristol REs to carry bodies featuring just a front entrance/exit was the batch numbered 2461–80. Number 2464 is seen here at Carr's Glen, with the lower slopes of the Cave Hill in the background. Note, too, the Belfast Corporation bus stops, that on the left-hand side of the road being mounted on a leaning trolleybus pole.
Paul Savage

A further follow up order for 150 vehicles was placed but this time only 35 were allocated to the Citybus fleet. Twenty, Nos 2211–30 (ROI 2211–30), were to the same configuration as the previous batches and were placed in service during 1978. The remaining 15 vehicles, Nos 2306–20 (TOI 2306–20), had single-door bodies, with seating for 50. These vehicles were also intended for use on private hire work and consequently were trimmed with soft seating. The four speed gearboxes fitted to these vehicles greatly reduced the overall speed and made them unpopular with drivers, especially on long private hire journeys. When the first of the second-hand REs arrived from Crosville and United in 1980, the opportunity was taken to exchange the five speed units fitted to those vehicles for the four speed units in the private hire batch.

British Leyland were by now unwilling to accept any further orders for the Bristol RE, but in a somewhat strange twist, they agreed to extend the previous order for 150 by a further 140. This order was split equally between Citybus and Ulsterbus, each receiving 70 in two batches of 40 and 30. Fleet nos 2321–60 (UOI 2321–60) and 2401–30 (VOI 8401–30) were delivered in 1979/80 and were fitted with the standard 32-seat dual-door bodies. Numbers 2328/35/8/48/50 (UOI 2328/35/8/48/50) and 2401–30 (VOI 8401–30) had a number of minor detail differences from the previous batches.

A further extension of 70 vehicles to the original order was accepted but in this instance, all were allocated to the Citybus fleet. Following safety issues relating to the centre exit on dual-door vehicles, it was decided that this feature would be dropped on all future orders. Numbers 2461–80 (WOI 8461–80) and 2481–2530 (XOI 2481–2530) were delivered in 1981/2 as 39-seaters, but many spent long periods in secure storage before being placed in traffic. The final vehicles of this order did not enter service until February 1984, two years after they were delivered. In addition, many of those placed in traffic were taken out of service, sometimes more than once, and placed in secure storage. This was to protect them during periods of high risk, particularly over the summer months.

One final extension to the original order was accepted, this time for a further 70 vehicles, of which 50 were allocated to the Citybus fleet. Fleet numbers 2531–60 (AXI 2531–60) were similar to the previous batch and were delivered between 1984 and 1986. The 20 remaining vehicles were built as soft seated examples with seating for 52 for use on private hire duties. Like the previous batch of such vehicles, these were fitted with the standard Gardner 6HLXB engine but this time it was rated at 150 bhp and coupled to a five speed semi automatic gearbox, giving them a better turn of speed. Fleet numbers 2561–80 (BXI 2561–80) were delivered in 1983/4 but, again, many were placed in secure storage, the final examples not entering service until June 1985.

In all 340 Bristol REs were delivered new to Citybus between 1976 and 1984 and they were to prove a most reliable and popular vehicle, the last examples surviving in service until 31 January 2004. Few problems were encountered with the type and as a result few chassis modifications were made.

Poor brake lining life was one problem associated with the Bristol RE, caused partially by poor weight distribution – approximately one third on the front axle and two thirds on the rear. It was normal to get 30,000 miles from the front lining but only 8,000–10,000 miles from the rear linings. Various measures were tried to transfer braking from the rear to the front but these tended to create more problems than they solved. In a relatively simple modification, Citybus managed to double brake lining life by fitting an electric fan connected to trunking that directed cool air onto the brake drum assemblies.

Rear spring failure tended to occur at around 50,000 miles and was generally not confined to one or two leaves, three or four often failing at once. In addition the Bristol RE was not fitted with rear shock absorbers which led to complaints from passengers about rough riding qualities, especially when the vehicles were lightly loaded. In an effort to provide a more comfortable ride and increase spring lift, Citybus turned to the British Steel Corporation Light Products Division for help. Fleet No 2524 (XOI 2524) was experimentally fitted with Taperlite springs at the British Steel Corporation plant in Sheffield in January 1984. Following trials on the mainland, No 2524 returned to Belfast in March 1984 and re-entered service the following month. The ride quality and the spring life were significantly improved by this modification, which also included the fitting of rear shock absorbers. A programme to retrofit all of the newer single-door Bristol REs with Taperlite springs was undertaken and even a few of the older dual-door vehicles, and a number of Ulsterbus vehicles, also received this modification.

Few modifications were carried out to the body of the Bristol REs during their service life. Following delivery of the second batch of private hire vehicles in 1982/3, ten of the original batch had their upholstered seats removed and replaced by glass fibre. Following repositioning of ticketing equipment in the dual-door vehicles, it was possible to fit a bench seat for three over the front nearside wheelarch increasing the capacity of the vehicles to 35. This was carried out in a somewhat haphazard fashion and only Nos 2045/62 (LOI 2045/62), 2086 (MOI 8086), 2103/12 (MOI 8103/12), 2137/8/41/3–5/8/51/3/8 (POI 2137/8/41/3–5/8/51/3/8), 2219/21/3/4 (ROI 2219/21/3/4), 2326/8/34–6/8/40/3/4/7 (UOI 2326/8/34–6/8/40/3/4/7) and 2401/2/5–7/12/3/25 (VOI 8401/2/5–7/12/3/25) are recorded as having received this modification, mainly during 1982.

Number 2059 (LOI 2059) was badly damaged after being hijacked and set on fire on 15 June 1984. It was subsequently used by Citybus Engineering as an apprentice training exercise and was rebuilt virtually from the floor up at their Falls Park workshops. It finally returned to service in September 1986, also reseated to 35.

Stone throwing attacks on vehicles had been a problem for many years, especially in the evenings and in the hours of darkness. Although really outside the period covered by this volume, a number of Bristol REs were fitted with impact resistant glass windscreens during 1994/5 in an effort to provide some additional protection to drivers. In order to fit the four piece windscreens to these vehicles, it was necessary to first fit a special, purpose made, frame to accommodate the glazing units. This modification did nothing to improve the appearance of the vehicles but made life a lot safer for drivers. Vehicles receiving this modification were Nos 2466/7/80 (WOI 8466/7/80), 2486/90/6/8 (XOI 2486/90/6/8), 2500/3/5–12/4–6/9/22–4 (XOI 2500/3/5–12/4–6/9/22–4), 2553/6/7/9 (AXI 2553/6/7/9) and 2576 (BXI 2576). It was planned to modify several other vehicles, including the last RE delivered, No 2580 (BXI 2580), but nothing ever came of this.

Over the years a number of vehicles lost their galvanised steel bumpers both front and rear, giving them a quite unusual appearance. Among the vehicles so modified were Nos 2060 (LOI 2060), 2141/4 (POI 2141/4) and 2342 (UOI 2342).

To provide drivers with some protection from stone throwing youths a number of Bristol REs were fitted with flat, impact resistant glass windscreens in the mid 1990s. The appearance of the vehicles so fitted was much different as additional framing was required to support the additional weight of the glass. This shot shows No 2506 in a later, and even then nonstandard, version of Citybus livery. *Raymond Bell*

Testing times

Northern Ireland had not been the only market reluctant to accept the integral Leyland National. Several important overseas markets prohibited the import of complete vehicles in order to protect the local coachbuilding industry and in some cases would not even allow vehicles to be imported in kit form. In an effort to overcome this, in 1974 Leyland Motors took the standard Leyland National sub-frame and running units and had Eastern Coach Works construct a body. The body incorporated the standard Leyland National front and rear ends but the remainder of the vehicle closely resembled the standard ECW aluminium framed bus shell under construction at that time. Known as the C27, it was only a matter of months before the project was taken one stage further and the B21 was born. A separate lightweight chassis was developed to incorporate the Leyland National running units and the radiator was moved to the front to improve cooling in tropical countries. Because of the lightweight nature of the chassis, it was necessary for the B21 to take much of its rigidity from the body structure. To this end, Leyland Motors produced a manual to assist coachbuilders with the design of suitable bodies. Although it had been on offer since 1974, it was to be 1980 before volume production of the type commenced and all initial orders were for overseas customers.

With production of the Bristol RE finally coming to an end, Leyland Motors were keen to encourage Ulsterbus and Citybus to take the B21. Eventually it was agreed that a fleet of six vehicles would be taken for evaluation, to be split equally between both companies. All were to be bodied by Alexander (Belfast) and the first vehicle appeared in 1980. Allocated fleet number 3000 and registered WOI 607, it was initially sent to England for pavé and other tests. Powered by a Leyland 690 engine developing 170 bhp at 2000rpm coupled to a five speed hydracyclic gearbox with built in retarder, it was fitted with a 44-seat dual-door body and was allocated to the Ulsterbus fleet. The main reason for the dual-door body layout was to put maximum stress on the body structure during the pavé testing. On its return from England, it was sent back to Alexander's where it was virtually rebuilt before finally entering service in February 1982. Rather surprisingly it retained its dual-door body layout but was re-engined with the more modern Leyland TL11 engine rated at 175 bhp at 1850 rpm.

The remaining five vehicles entered service in 1981/2, with Nos 3001/5 (WOI 3001/5) being allocated to the Ulsterbus fleet and Nos 3002–4 (WOI 3002–4) going to the Citybus fleet. Numbers 3001–3 (WOI 3001–3) were fitted with Leyland TL11 engines, rated at 170 bhp at 2000rpm, coupled to five speed pneumocyclic gearboxes. All had single-door bodies, Nos 3001/3 seating 53 and No 3002 seating 43. The other two vehicles were fitted with Gardner 6HLXB engines coupled to five speed pneumocyclic gearboxes. Number 3004 had its engine rated at 135 bhp at 1700 rpm whilst No 3005 had its engine uprated to 150 bhp at 1850 rpm. Both, once again, had single-door bodies, No 3004 having a 33-seat standee layout and No 3005 having seating for 53. Number 3004 was upseated to 42 in 1990 and further upseated to 46 later in the same year. In 1989 No 3005 was transferred to join sister No 3004 in the Citybus fleet.

These vehicles failed to impress and no further orders followed. Indeed only four other Leyland B21s were built for the domestic market. These were constructed for Ipswich Buses in 1984 and, like the earlier examples, were bodied at the Alexander (Belfast) plant, but this time with the 'N' type body more traditionally associated with the Leyland Tiger. Despite being nonstandard, the local B21s survived until 1991 when all were withdrawn and sold to Ipswich Buses thus bringing all ten of the type into one fleet. They went on to have long lives with their new owners and the last examples were not withdrawn until 2004.

Leyland were keen for Citybus/Ulsterbus to take its B21 model as the replacement for the Bristol RE and a batch of six, with Alexander (Belfast) bodies, were taken for evaluation in 1981/2. Number 3000 underwent a series of punishing tests in England before returning to Alexander's where it was rebuilt. It is seen here at Ulsterbus' Duncrue Street works prior to entering service with Ulsterbus at Larne. Alongside is Ulsterbus B21 No 3005, which was transferred to Citybus in 1989.

Raymond Bell

Before a new type of vehicle can enter public service it must undergo a series of stringent tests, one of which involves being tilted. Double-deckers must achieve an angle of 28° from the horizontal and single-deckers 35°. Citybus is able to undertake tilt tests at its Falls Park workshops and here Leyland B21 No 3003 is pictured undergoing such a test and reaching an angle of 37°.
Paul Savage collection

By the early 1980s, Leyland Motors were looking to replace the now ageing Leyland National with a new model. To this end a low floor single-deck rear-engined bus chassis was developed, initially for the export market, but from 1986 was to be offered as a complete integral vehicle for the domestic market. Initially a choice of two engines was available, the Leyland TL11 and the Gardner 6LXB, although the latter was soon replaced by the 6LXCT engine. Later two further engine options were offered – the Cummins L10 and the Volvo THD 0102. Gearbox options were the Leyland hydracyclic four speed semi-automatic gearbox with fluid coupling or the Leyland hydracyclic four speed fully-automatic gearbox with torque coupling. Options offered later were the Voith D851 or the ZF HP500. Following Leyland's passion for naming their vehicles after big cats, this new model was christened Lynx.

Citybus and Ulsterbus agreed to take a trial batch of seven vehicles for evaluation purposes and during early 1984, one of the initial batch of six pre-production chassis was delivered to Alexander (Belfast) for bodying. It was fitted with a 37-seat dual-door body based on the 'N' type design which had been developed for the Ulsterbus Leyland Tiger. The Gardner 6LXB engine, coupled to the Leyland four speed fully-automatic gearbox, powered the prototype vehicle. It was allocated to the Citybus fleet as No 3006 and was registered HXI 3006, but instead of being placed in traffic it was sent to the MIRA test track at

Nuneaton in June 1984 for extensive pavé testing to be undertaken. Once the testing was complete, it was returned to the Alexander (Belfast) plant where it was extensively rebuilt. During this rebuild the centre exit was removed and it finally entered service in December 1985 as a 37-seat single-door vehicle. It returned to England once more in October 1986 where its fully automatic transmission was replaced by a Leyland four speed semi-automatic unit.

The remaining six chassis were delivered to Alexander (Belfast) in 1986 and emerged later that year as fleet numbers 3007–12 (HXI 3007–12). The first four were allocated to the Citybus fleet. Numbers 3007–9 were powered by the Gardner 6LXB engine whilst 3010–12 had the Leyland TL11 engine, all with the Leyland four speed semi-automatic gearbox. Numbers 3007–10 all seated 43 when new, the other two vehicles having 53 seats. In June 1987 Nos 3007–10 were downseated to 38 and repainted in an allover advertising livery for use on the Northern Ireland Railways *Rail-Link* service. The two Ulsterbus vehicles were to join the Citybus fleet in 1989.

As with the Leyland B21, the Lynx failed to find favour in Northern Ireland and after a service life of just over five years, all were withdrawn and sold to a mainland operator. Interestingly five of the batch were later to return to Ireland with operators in the private sector and at the time of writing (February 2005), one is still operating on schools traffic for an operator in Co Tyrone.

After the Leyland B21 Citybus evaluated the Leyland Lynx, the first, No 3006, entering service in December 1985, with the rest following in 1986 – four to Citybus and two to Ulsterbus, although these were transferred to Citybus later. Much like the B21 the Lynx didn't find favour in Northern Ireland and the seven vehicles were sold to an English operator, Stevenson's, in 1991. They led full lives and five later returned to Ireland for further use – four with Keenan, Bellurgan Point, Co Louth and one (No 3007) with McGread of Omagh, Co Tyrone.   *Paul Rafferty*

Enter the big cats

With both the Leyland B21 and Lynx having failed to impress, it became necessary to seek out an alternative vehicle type for the Citybus fleet replacement programme. Ulsterbus had adopted the Leyland Tiger with Alexander (Belfast) 'N' type body for its service bus and express coach needs. Most were powered by the Leyland TL11 engine, but one of the initial batch of 40 had been fitted with a Gardner 6LXC engine for evaluation. Ulsterbus placed no further orders for this engine option, but a batch of ten were ordered for the Citybus fleet. Fleet Nos 2601–10 (LXI 6610–10) were delivered in 1988 and as with the Ulsterbus vehicles, were fitted with the Alexander 'N' type body but with the seating capacity reduced to 43. Of the initial batch, Nos 2601/10 were fitted with Taperlite springs, the remainder having standard air suspension. All of these vehicles were later fitted with armoured windscreens to provide greater protection for drivers in stone throwing attacks, an all too common pastime in certain parts of Belfast. The initial order for ten was quickly followed up by a further order for 25 of the type, Nos 2611–35 (NXI 4611–35), which were delivered in late 1988/early 1989.

More information on the Citybus Leyland Tigers will appear in *Buses in Ulster*, Volume 6.

After trying the Leyland B21 and Leyland Lynx, in 1988 Citybus turned to what had been the Ulsterbus standard for several years, the Leyland Tiger. The Citybus Tigers featured Gardner engines (Leyland TL11 in Ulsterbus examples), a lower floor line in the front part of the saloon and low profile tyres to reduce the step height. Tiger No 2601 is seen in Donegall Square West in 1988 when brand new. The building directly behind the bus is the Northern Bank, now famous for the robbery which took place there in December 2004. Marshall's Coffee Shop, well known to busmen, closed in 2004 and is now an upmarket clothes shop.
Paul Savage

The Troubles

The outbreak of civil disturbances in 1969 was to have a major effect on bus services throughout Northern Ireland, especially in the cities of Belfast and Londonderry. Rioting was commonplace and vehicles were frequently seized by mobs to form barricades, thus protecting themselves from rival mobs or the authorities. Many of these vehicles were subsequently set on fire making them an even more effective deterrent.

The size and availability of buses made them a popular choice for barricades and between the outbreak of the Troubles in 1969 and the formation of Citybus in 1973, approximately 100 vehicles in the Belfast Corporation Transport fleet were destroyed, with countless more suffering damage. As time progressed events were to take a more sinister turn with vehicles being specifically targeted. Frequently buses were simply stopped by mobs, some of which were armed, and after the driver and passengers had been ordered off, the vehicle was set on fire. In addition, depot installations were firebombed resulting in large numbers of vehicles being destroyed at a time. Between 1973 and 1987 approximately 500 more vehicles were to be destroyed, averaging 32 a year. 1975 was to be a quiet year with only eight vehicles destroyed. 1977 was to be the worst year when 79 were destroyed closely followed by 1980 when 60 were lost. The worst single incident took place on 18 January 1979 when the bus park at the rear of Falls Park depot was firebombed resulting in the loss of 24 vehicles. However February 1980 was to be the worst single month for losses with no fewer than 40 vehicles being destroyed. A firebomb attack on Falls Park depot on 1 February claimed 19 vehicles and a similar attack on Ardoyne depot on 29 February claimed a further 21 vehicles. Ardoyne was to be attacked again in July 1980 with the loss of eight vehicles and once again in December, when a further three vehicles were destroyed.

Changing social trends and ever increasing car ownership were already seeing a big reduction in public transport usage. The worsening situation on the streets saw a further drop in usage, especially at nights and weekends. Rioting and hijacking led to services having to be curtailed or suspended altogether in parts of Belfast, sometimes for considerable periods. Bomb attacks and bomb hoaxes caused considerable disruption to services, with routes having to be diverted and from time to time depots had to be temporarily vacated for the safety of both vehicles and staff.

Many members of staff suffered injury, sometimes serious, during the Troubles and between 1972 and 1986 four members of Citybus staff and eight members of Ulsterbus staff were to lose their lives in the course of their duties. In 1996 a memorial panel to those who died was erected at Laganside Buscentre (see picture overleaf).

The wording on the adjacent plaque reads:

> This ceramic panel is a memorial to the staff of Ulsterbus and Citybus who were killed in the course of their duties during the Troubles. The names of the twelve who died are shown on the buses enclosing the lower section of the design.
>
> The upper half of the panel representing Belfast includes the old Oxford Street Bus Station, whilst the lower half represents town and country services throughout the province. Dividing the two sections is a river representing the journey from one life to another.
>
> Designed and crafted by Diane McCormick, the panel was formally unveiled by Neville Whitehead, Chairman of Citybus, Northern Ireland Railways and Ulsterbus, on the occasion of the opening of Laganside Buscentre on 1 May 1996.

Citybus staff:		Ulsterbus staff:	
S Agnew	1972	T Callaghan	1972
P Crossan	1973	WK Crothers	1972
A Millar	1975	J Gibson	1972
H Bradshaw	1977	WH Irvine	1972
		T Killops	1972
		S Rush	1973
		D McDowell	1976
		J Gibson	1982

As already mentioned, Daimler Fleetline No 2857 (EOI 4857), which had been rebodied by Alexander (Belfast) in 1976 after itself having been a victim of the Troubles, was restored on withdrawal and presented to the Ulster Folk & Transport Museum at Cultra as a permanent memorial to the staff who died.

This troubled period will be looked at in greater detail in a later book.

Opposite: In April 1974 the operations of Coastal Bus Services Ltd, Portrush, were taken over by Ulsterbus. Amongst the vehicles acquired were two Daimler Roadliners, a type Citybus engineers had got to know very well. Given fleet numbers 1298 and 1299, only the latter was to see use and entered service in December 1974 (and being a Roadliner it probably expired very shortly after). In this view we see it at Short Strand depot, where, rumour has it, it spent most of its time. Daimler Fleetline double-deckers and AEC Swift single-deckers are also to be seen. *Raymond Bell*

Troubled times – the second-hand acquisitions

Second-hand vehicles had never formed a major part of the Belfast Corporation Transport fleet and it had been almost twenty years since any second-hand additions had been made to this fleet.

The first second-hand vehicles to be added to the Citybus fleet were two Marshall-bodied Daimler Roadliners, which had been acquired by Ulsterbus Ltd in April 1974 with the fleet and operations of Robinson, Portrush (t/a Coastal Bus Services Ltd). Numbers 1298 (KVT 175E) and 1299 (7901 YZ, ex KVT 175E) had been Nos 22 and 21 respectively in the Coastal fleet, although the former had yet to be used by them. They were part of a batch of five similar vehicles acquired by Coastal from Potteries Motor Traction, Stoke on Trent. Only two had arrived in Northern Ireland at the time of the takeover and the remaining three vehicles were subsequently scrapped on the mainland. Given that Citybus were already operating Roadliners it made sense to transfer these two vehicles to the Citybus operation. In the event only one was to see use, No 1298 being used as a source of spare parts at Falls Park depot before being sold for scrap. Number 1299 was finally placed in service in December 1974 but proved to be no more reliable than its native sister vehicles and led a somewhat nomadic existence. It was used very much as a vehicle of last resort and spent long periods parked up out of use. It was finally withdrawn in 1976 and sold for scrap.

A further former Coastal vehicle was added to the fleet in September 1975 when Marshall-bodied AEC Swift No 1300 (CIA 3000, ex LYY 827D) was transferred from the Ulsterbus fleet. On the takeover of Coastal by Ulsterbus Ltd, this vehicle was allocated to Londonderry for use on the city services but was withdrawn at the end of June 1974 after only three months use. After a period in store it was transferred to the Citybus fleet who already operated a batch of AEC Swifts. It was never used in service and was sold to an operator in the Republic of Ireland in 1976. This vehicle had originally been an AEC demonstrator and had been used by Ulsterbus in late 1967 in comparative trials with an ECW-bodied Bristol RE. It was subsequently sold to Antrim County Council for use as a staff bus but after the second of two serious accidents, it was sold to Coastal who subsequently repaired it and placed it in service as their fleet No 6. During the repairs its centre exit door was sealed and the stepwell infilled, features it was to retain for the rest of its operating life.

Serious vehicle shortages during 1974 saw the first transfers of Ulsterbus vehicles to the Citybus fleet. Between March and October 1974, no fewer than 24 Leyland Tiger Cubs with Weymann 43-seat bodies were acquired, although in the event only 18 were placed in service. New to Edinburgh Corporation in 1959, 48 of the vehicles were purchased by the Ulster Transport Authority in 1966 to help improve the age profile of the fleet and to help eliminate the half cab rear entrance single-decker, which was not suitable for one man operation. Although built for and operated on city services, the narrow entrance door and high floor line did not make them particularly suited for use on Citybus services. Whilst they did venture out on service from time to time, they tended to be confined to schools duties and private hire work. All of these vehicles retained Ulsterbus livery during their time with Citybus but with the addition of Citybus fleetnames in red lettering on a yellow background, which were applied to the front and side panels.

Between January and June 1975 a further eight of the Leyland Tiger Cubs were transferred in from Ulsterbus, seven of which were used in service. More unusual additions were two Ulsterbus Leyland Titan PD3/5 double-deckers which were fitted with UTA FH39/28F bodies. Although Ulsterbus had been using this type of vehicle on one man operated services, they were far from suitable for this role. Although equipped with a front entrance, the door was situated behind the front axle and in order to collect fares and issue tickets, the driver had to turn right round in his seat. These vehicles tended to be confined to schools duties and driver training work, where fare collection was not required. As with the Leyland Tiger Cubs, both retained Ulsterbus livery during their short time with Citybus. Both lasted only a matter of months and were withdrawn by the end of 1975.

Vehicle shortages in 1974 saw the transfer of a number of ex-Edinburgh Corporation Leyland Tiger Cubs to Citybus. None were repainted from blue to red, so were fitted with yellow vinyls, with **CITYBUS** in red lettering, to distinguish them from Ulsterbus vehicles. They were not really suited to city work and spent most of their time on schools and contract duties. Number 1027 is seen here on such duties outside the Corporation swimming baths at Ormeau Avenue. Just visible on this vehicle, about half way along its length, is a short line, painted yellow. This was to indicate the floor line to the Army's bomb disposal teams when they were called upon to deal with suspect packages left on vehicles.

Raymond Bell

January 1977 saw a further five of the Leyland Tiger Cubs transferred from Ulsterbus, three of which were used in service. The nine vehicles not used in service were used as a source of spare parts to keep the others in traffic. Withdrawal of these vehicles commenced in 1974, with the last going in 1977.

The serious vehicle losses suffered by Citybus in late 1976/early 1977 led to the company to look around for a source of second-hand vehicles to help bolster the fleet. One operator who at the time had a considerable number of surplus buses was London Transport and in February 1977, a batch of 20 AEC Merlins with Metro-Cammell-Weymann 50-seat single door bodies arrived. This was not the first time second-hand vehicles had come from this source, a batch of 100 Daimler CWA6s with wartime utility bodies having been purchased by Belfast Corporation Transport Dept in the early 1950s for tramway replacement.

The AEC Merlin was a product of the mid-1960s when ever rising costs, coupled with staff shortages, saw many operators seek methods of addressing these problems. One solution was to eliminate the use of conductors and to introduce one man operation. Traditional open platform rear entrance double-deckers were of course unsuitable for conversion and the new generation of rear-engined front entrance double-deckers were not legally permitted to be used as one man operated vehicles at this time. Indeed the range of single-deck vehicles available at this time was not particularly suited for use as high capacity one man operated vehicles. One man operated single-deck city service vehicles were common on the continent but had never enjoyed much success in the United Kingdom. As no such vehicles were readily available on the home market, manufacturers had to develop a vehicle from scratch. What was needed was a 36'0" long vehicle, the maximum permissible at this time, and in order to keep the floor line as low as possible the engine had to be repositioned to the rear.

One of the first batch of former London Transport 'MB class' AEC Merlins was No 2532, seen here in Upper Queen Street. Ex-London Transport vehicles had operated in Belfast previously; 100 Daimler CWA6s were acquired by the Corporation in 1953 to help speed up tramway replacement. One of the batch, No 476, has been preserved. More information on/pictures of the CWAs can be found in *Buses in Ulster*, Volume 3. *Paul Savage*

Daimler initially produced the Cummins-engined Roadliner chassis which was to prove to be a total disaster. Citybus had experience of the type, having inherited a batch with the fleet of Belfast Corporation Transport Dept. In addition it had also obtained the two examples which had been acquired when Ulsterbus Ltd took over the fleet and operations of Coastal Bus Services, Portrush. Following the problems with the Roadliner, Daimler produced a single-deck version of their highly successful Fleetline double-deck bus but as it transpired, these were not without their problems either.

By now AEC and Leyland, two of the biggest players in the market, had combined forces and in order to satisfy their respective markets, had developed two vehicles that shared a common chassis frame. One was powered by Leyland units and became the Leyland Panther. The other was fitted with the 11.3 litre AEC AH691 engine rated at 147bhp at 1800rpm mounted horizontally behind the rear axle and was to become the AEC Merlin. This name was subsequently dropped in favour of AEC Swift although London Transport continued to refer to them as Merlins.

London Transport had traditionally been an AEC operator and consequently ordered an experimental batch of 15 Merlins which were to be bodied by Strachans, a body builder not normally associated with London. These entered service in 1966 but before any significant operational feedback could be obtained, a follow up order for 650 vehicles was placed. The chassis was an improved type incorporating modifications designed to eliminate weaknesses in the original design. It retained the same AEC AH691 engine but this time rated at 165bhp. This time the body order was placed with Metro-Cammell-Weymann of Birmingham and contained a mixture of single and dual door vehicles for use on both suburban and country operations.

A total of 108 vehicles were allocated to the country fleet, all being dual door vehicles. Seventy-five were of the 25-seat standee variety and were classified 'MBS' whilst the remainder were 45-seat country vehicles and were classified 'MB'. On the formation of the National Bus Company in 1970, all of these vehicles passed to the newly formed London Country Bus Services. The 'MBS' vehicles were reseated to 33 in 1971 and vehicles of both types were subsequently added to the Citybus fleet in 1979/80. The remaining 542 vehicles were for use in central London and were of three basic types. Three hundred and forty-five were dual door standee vehicles seating 25. Of these, 302 vehicles were suburban flat fare vehicles classified 'MBS', the remaining 44 being for use on *Red Arrow* services in central London and classified 'MBA'. Some 'MBS' vehicles were later modified for use on the *Red Arrow* services being reclassified 'MBA'. The remaining 196 vehicles had 50-seat single door bodies and were classified 'MB'.

One major problem that quickly became apparent was the lack of rigidity in the chassis frame. Strachans had catered for this when building the experimental vehicles but this had not been taken on board by Metro-Cammell-Weymann. Most buses being built at this time utilised aluminium framing but for the Merlins the older and more traditional method of steel channel with wood inserts was used, leading to a weaker form of construction. The dual door layout, coupled with the chassis flexing, resulted in distortion and cracking of the body structure especially around the centre exit, a weak spot on dual door vehicles anyway. These cracks allowed water ingress into the body structure shorting out electrics and leading to all sorts of problems. Body distortion also caused the centre doors to jam in the open position at which point safety interlocks came into play preventing gears from being engaged. What little seating there was in the dual door vehicles was at the rear behind the back axle. In addition to accentuating the cracking problems around the centre exit, it also caused weight distribution problems and made the vehicles somewhat unstable in service.

The Merlins were packed with innovative features, many of which just added to their problems. Automatic fare collection equipment on standee vehicles proved troublesome, either jamming or failing to dispense tickets or change. With the standee vehicles drivers had difficulty observing the centre exit and ensuring it was free of alighting passengers before the doors were closed. To overcome this a photo electric light beam was installed across the centre exit. Passengers alighting from the vehicle broke the beam and prevented the doors being closed. On the standee buses, especially at peak times, passengers would inadvertently break the beam and immobilise the vehicle. Eventually the automatic fare collection equipment had to be removed along with the light beams and a simple system of mirrors was installed to allow the driver to observe the centre exit. Fitting external plates at cantrail level to all body pillars also strengthened the basic body structure.

By 1971 availability was at an all time low. Spare parts were hard to come by and it was not uncommon to wait up to 12 months for certain items. Things were so bad that at one time 20% of the fleet was out of traffic. The original Certificates of Fitness for the prototype batch were due to expire in 1973. In June 1972 one of the batch was taken in for a pilot overhaul which took eight months to complete. By the time it reappeared only two of the prototypes still remained in traffic and these were withdrawn shortly afterwards. The cost and time taken to overhaul the prototype Merlins was considered excessive and it was decided that no more would be done. Overhauls on the production vehicles were due to commence in 1975 but given all the problems that had been encountered with these vehicles, authority was sought to replace them. By now one man operation of double-deck vehicles had been legalised and in August 1973 authority was given to replace the Merlin fleet using a mixture of new double-deck vehicles and by extending the lives of older and more reliable vehicles. Withdrawals commenced in 1973 although in reality many of those withdrawn had already been out of service for a considerable period of time.

Being relatively young vehicles, London Transport was obviously keen to try and sell many of them. However given their somewhat dubious reliability record and coupled with the fact that many operators were switching back to double-deckers, now that one man operation of the type had been legalised, resulted in few sales. Storage of such a large number of vehicles proved to be a problem. In 1975 space was rented at the disused Radlett Aerodrome and by the end of the year over 300 Merlins were there. Sales had seen a number of vehicles exported for further use in Africa and Australia whereas domestic sales were generally confined to non-PSV operators, many for use as airside buses at various airports. A few even operated at Belfast City Airport for a short time before being replaced by Leyland Nationals. In 1977 the Radlett site was sold for redevelopment and London Transport had little option but to dispatch large numbers of the unloved and unwanted vehicles to the Yorkshire breakers for scrapping.

The first batch of vehicles to arrive in Belfast was of the 'MB' single door type and dated from 1968. Allocated fleet numbers 2531–50, all were rapidly placed in service still in London Transport livery, not being repainted into Citybus livery until the immediate crisis subsided. Citybus drivers collected all from London over the weekend of 19/20 February 1977. Few modifications were carried out before the vehicles were placed in traffic, the only major one being the removal of a single seat to allow the fitting of ticket equipment. Between September 1978 and August 1981, no fewer than eight of the batch were to become victims of the troubles. Number 2547 (AML 654H) was withdrawn in October 1981 after suffering accident damage. Number 2542 (AML 644H) was the first 'normal' withdrawal of the batch in October 1980. The remainder were withdrawn in 1981 and 1982, some giving a creditable five years service with their new owner.

A second batch of ten vehicles was acquired in March 1977. Eight were of the 'MBS' standee type and were allocated fleet numbers 2523–30. All were placed in service during May/June 1977 but by the end of the year no fewer than five had been hijacked and destroyed. A further vehicle was to meet the same fate in April 1981. Number 2523 (VLW 207G) was withdrawn in June 1980, leaving No 2528 (VLW 222G) as the sole survivor. In order to release the fleet number for use on a new vehicle, it was renumbered to 675 in September 1981 and was finally withdrawn the following month. The remaining two vehicles of the batch were of the 'MB' type and were allocated fleet numbers 2521/2. However instead of entering service with Citybus, both were allocated to the Ulsterbus fleet. Number 2522 (VLW 366G) was eventually transferred to the Citybus fleet in March 1980, surviving almost eighteen months in service before being hijacked and destroyed.

May 1977 saw the arrival of a further batch of 10 'MB' type vehicles, followed by another five similar vehicles in July. Allocated fleet numbers 2506–20, once again all were allocated to the Ulsterbus fleet. Numbers 2511–3/7/8 (VLW 346/52/3/64/87G) were subsequently transferred to the Citybus fleet in March 1980 to be followed by No 2508 (VLW 370G) two months later. Of these Nos 2513 (VLW 353G) and 2518 (VLW 387G) were hijacked and destroyed in August and May 1981 respectively. Number 2508 was withdrawn in October 1980 to be followed by No 2512 (VLW 352G) in April the following year. Numbers 2511/7 were renumbered 673/4 in September 1981 to release the fleet numbers for new vehicles. Both survived until March 1982, No 674 being withdrawn after suffering malicious damage. Number 673 was one of the batch later sold to a mainland breaker for scrapping.

In September 1977 a further batch of eight vehicles arrived but this time they were of the 'MBA' type, latterly used on *Red Arrow* services. Allocated fleet numbers 2498–2505, all were placed in service in November/December 1977. Following a disastrous firebomb attack on the Ulsterbus depot at Pennyburn in Londonderry in February 1978, Nos 2500–3/5 (AML 572/86, 603/4/13H) were hastily dispatched to Ulsterbus to help maintain services. All returned to the Citybus fleet in April 1978 with the exception of No 2502 which did not return until September. Between April 1978 and December 1980, six of the batch were to fall victim of the troubles leaving only Nos 2498 and 2502. These were subsequently renumbered 671/2 in September 1981 to release fleet numbers for new vehicles, both being withdrawn by the end of the year. Number 672 went the same way as No 673, being sold to a breaker in England.

The final AEC Merlins received from London Transport arrived in November 1977 and were of the 'MBA' standee type. Allocated fleet numbers 2489–97, all were initially prepared for service before being placed in store. Vehicle shortages in the Ulsterbus fleet saw five, including No 2497, transferred without being used. Number 2497 later returned to Belfast, in March 1980 and entered service with Citybus. In this view it is parked on the forecourt of Falls Park depot, straddling the tram lines. Although trams had ceased to operate on the Falls Road in 1938 the rails were still in-situ in the depot up until the 1980s and some are still in place in the workshop area in 2005! *Paul Savage*

A final batch of nine Merlins was received from London Transport in November 1977 and was once again were of the 'MBA' standee type. Allocated fleet numbers 2489–97, all were initially prepared for service before being placed in store. Serious vehicle shortages in the Ulsterbus fleet saw Nos 2490–2/4 (VLW 460/1/5, 527G) and 2497 (AML 576H) transferred to Ulsterbus without being used. Of these No 2494 was destroyed in October 1978 and Nos 2491/2 were withdrawn and scrapped in late 1980. Numbers 2490 and 2497 returned to the Citybus fleet in March 1980, No 2490 (VLW 460G) subsequently being destroyed in December of the same year. Number 2497 (AML 576H) was renumbered 670 in September 1981 to release the fleet number for a new vehicle. It was withdrawn two months later and subsequently returned to a mainland breaker for scrapping. The four remaining vehicles of this batch, Nos 2489/93/5 (VLW 454, 518/46G) and 2496 (AML 548H), were taxed as private vehicles rather than PSVs from 1 April 1978 for use as mobile offices to facilitate the issue of concessionary passes to the over 65s. On completion of these duties in November 1978, all were returned to store. Number 2495 was returned to Citybus and placed in service in December 1978 only to be hijacked and destroyed eight months later. The remaining three were never to see passenger service. Numbers 2489/93 were used as a source of spare parts before being scrapped whilst No 2496 was destroyed in a firebomb attack on the Ulsterbus depot at Pennyburn, Londonderry in December 1978.

Despite all the problems London Transport had suffered with these vehicles, the Merlins were to serve Citybus well and helped the company maintain services through what were very difficult times.

In addition to the AEC Merlins, Citybus purchased a batch of 14 Daimler Fleetline single-deckers from Potteries Motor Traction, Stoke on Trent. These vehicles were a mere seven years old and were fitted with the Alexander (Falkirk) 'W' style dual-door body seating 41. Mechanically similar to native Nos 2773–2801 (AOI 773–801), they also shared the same basic body structure although in this case they had the much larger panoramic windows. Allocated fleet Nos 2920–33, these vehicles arrived in March 1977 and were quickly repainted and pressed into service over the next couple of months, being downseated to 40 at this time. The Citybus livery suited these vehicles well although their appearance was somewhat marred in later years by the fitting of simplified front panels. Despite being the worst possible combination of a dual-door rear engined vehicle with panoramic windows, these vehicles were popular and served Belfast well. Of the initial batch of 14 vehicles, seven were to meet a premature end as a result of the Troubles. The rest went on to give between five and six years service, the last example not being withdrawn until March 1983.

Following the arrival of Merlins Nos 2489–97 in November 1977, London Transport were not in a position to supply any further vehicles of this type. The remaining vehicles were being retained to operate the *Red Arrow* network of services, with a few others kept to provide a source of spare parts. However, Ulsterbus/Citybus managed to obtain a further five examples of the type in July 1977 purely as a source of spare parts. These came from Wombwell Diesels in Barnsley who had taken considerable numbers of Merlins for breaking. Two were allocated to Ulsterbus for breaking up, the other three being dismantled for spare parts by Citybus.

With no further London Transport AEC Merlins available, Citybus took up an option to purchase fifty AEC Swifts from the same source, an option later increased to 80. Fleet Nos 1–80 were allocated to these vehicles and by the end of 1978 a total of 68 of these vehicles had been collected, the remainder being received early in 1979.

The AEC Swifts were basically a smaller version of the AEC Merlin. Operational experience in London with the Merlins had revealed that the overall length and the long rear overhang on these vehicles were causing problems. Before delivery of the Merlins had been completed it was decided that future single-deck orders would be for the 33'5" long AEC Swift as opposed to the 36'0" long Merlin. The AEC AH691 engine used in the Merlin could not be used in the Swift due to the shorter rear overhang so the smaller 8.2 litre

Citybus had much experience with the Daimler Fleetline and when Potteries Motor Traction of Stoke on Trent had a batch of seven year old Alexander-bodied Fleetline single-deckers available they were eagerly snapped up. Number 2922, fitted with a later, plainer style of front panel, rests in Donegall Square West with a native Fleetline single-decker, No 2800, behind and an AEC Merlin, No 628, on the right. *Paul Savage*

capacity AEC AH505 engine was fitted instead. London Transport ordered 838 vehicles of this type although 138 were delivered direct to London Country Bus Services, Reigate who had taken over the 'country' operations of London Transport on formation of the National Bus Company on 1 January 1970. The first fifty vehicles of the type had 42-seat single-door bodies built by Marshall of Cambridge. The remainder of the London Transport vehicles were built as 33-seat dual-door buses. Three coachbuilders were chosen to construct the bodies on these vehicles – Park Royal, London (295), Metro-Cammell-Weymann, Birmingham (330) and Marshall, Cambridge (75). The bodies produced by all three companies were to a standard design with only minor detail differences. They entered service between January 1970 and March 1972, the single-door vehicles becoming the 'SM' class and the dual-door vehicles the 'SMS' class. Of the vehicles supplied directly to London Country 48 received 38-seat Park Royal dual-door bodies with the remaining 90 getting 41-seat dual-door bodies by Metro-Cammell-Weymann.

Mechanical reliability of the AEC Swift was not good and engine failures were a major problem with the type throughout their relatively short life with London Transport. The smaller higher revving engine fitted to these vehicles gave a smaller power output than the Merlins – 132 bhp as opposed to 165 bhp. Drivers complained that the Swifts were underpowered which was not in fact the case. The Swift was around half a ton lighter than the Merlin which actually gave a better power to weight ratio. Other mechanical problems encountered were with the heating and cooling systems and with the steering. Water leaks also became apparent in the bodies as well as serious cracking in the body and floor structures around the centre exit.

When London Transport was unable to supply further Merlins, Citybus purchased 80 of the shorter AEC Swift – 60 'SMS class' and 20 of the 'SMD class'. Number 18, the former SMS 608, had been pressed into use with Ulsterbus, following a depot fire at Smithfield, when caught by the photographer in the yard at Oxford Street depot. Little modification has been made to its London condition, even retaining the red and grey livery. *Author*

Despite there being three different bodybuilders involved in their construction, the structural problems were common to all types. Expensive repairs were necessary to remedy the body defects but the mechanical problems were never really successfully mastered.

In 1974 a need was identified for more conventional one man operated single-deckers and a programme was instigated to upseat some standee dual-door 'SMS' vehicles from 33 to 42, these vehicles being reclassified 'SMD'. Only Park Royal-bodied vehicles were chosen for conversion, the floors on the Marshall-bodied vehicles being unsuitable for fitting additional seats. In addition to the upseating, the central exit doors were permanently sealed and the stepwell infilled. A total of 104 such conversions was undertaken before the programme was abandoned.

Pilot overhauls were undertaken on examples from each batch and type in late 1974/early 1975 but the writing was already on the wall for the Swift. The availability of spare parts had always been a problem for both the Merlins and the Swifts and by the end of 1975 the situation was so bad that of the 700 Swifts operated by London Transport only 551 were scheduled for service at any one time, an availability rate of only 79%. The first official withdrawals of the type took place in October 1976 when 24 were withdrawn, although in reality most of these had been out of service for a considerable period of time. The following month London Transport announced that it was to replace the entire fleet of Swifts and over the next five years all were eliminated from the fleet.

Of the 80 vehicles purchased by Citybus, Nos 1–60 were of the 'SMS' type and Nos 61–80 were of the 'SMD' type. Four of the 'SMS' vehicles had bodies by Park Royal, six by Marshall and the remainder had Metro-Cammell-Weymann bodies. The first eight vehicles arrived in February 1978, the remainder being delivered in a further eight batches between April 1978 and May 1979. Of the initial batch of vehicles only four were to enter passenger service.

Early in 1978 both Citybus and Ulsterbus were making plans to issue concessionary passes to all those over 65 years of age, this scheme eventually coming on line on 3 July 1978. In order to facilitate the issuing of these passes, four stored AEC Merlins and four stored AEC Swifts were placed in use as mobile offices on 1 April 1978, these vehicles being taxed privately rather than as PSVs. Swifts Nos 1/8/9/10 and the previously mentioned Merlins Nos 2489/93/5/6 were chosen to fulfil this role. On completion of these duties in November 1978, all were once again returned to store.

Of the 80 vehicles purchased by Citybus, two of the 'SMS' type and 12 of the 'SMD' type were sold without being used. Of the eight 'SMD' type vehicles placed in service, seven continued to operate as 42-seaters with the centre doors sealed and the stepwell infilled. Fleet No 78 was downseated to 40 and had the centre exit door reinstated.

August 1979 saw the arrival of a further two Alexander-bodied dual-door Daimler Fleetline single-deckers from Potteries Motor Traction, Stoke-on-Trent. These were identical to the fourteen vehicles purchased from the same source earlier in the year and were allocated fleet Nos 2934/5. Number 2934 lasted a mere ten months before being hijacked and destroyed but No 2935 was to go on to give almost five years service.

A further batch of single-deck Daimler Fleetlines was acquired in March 1978, this time from Northern General, Gateshead. Allocated fleet Nos 2936–50, these vehicles differed from the earlier batch in that they were fitted with 44-seat Willowbrook dual-door bodies. New in 1972, these vehicles were part of a sizeable order placed by a number of National Bus Company operators. Bodies were to be built by Marshall or Willowbrook to a basically similar design. Major structural weaknesses in the body led a number of operators to embark on a programme of rebuilding the vehicles, which included the removal of the centre exit. The programme however was never completed and the unconverted vehicles were rapidly sold off, many for scrap. Even the rebuilt vehicles had relatively short lives, being dispensed with at the first opportunity. Following overhaul and repaint, these vehicles were placed in traffic by Citybus between May and October 1978. Sadly these vehicles fared little better in Belfast and rapidly set about shaking themselves to pieces. Of the batch of 15, a total of 10 were to be lost in street disturbances and attacks on depots, No 2939 (LCN 510K) lasting only ten days in service. Of the remainder, the first to go was No 2947 (LCN 522K) after just 18 months in service. The others succumbed rapidly, the last example being withdrawn in July 1981.

The poor reliability of the ex London Transport AEC Swifts led Citybus to look for an alternative source of vehicles. London Transport were unable to supply any more AEC Merlins at this time so they turned to London Country Bus Services, Reigate who also had three batches of these vehicles and was in the process of withdrawing them.

London Country was set up in 1970 on the formation of the National Bus Company to take over the rural operations of London Transport and included in the deal were 108 dual-door AEC Merlins of two basic types, the 45-seat 'MB class' and the 33-seat 'MBS class'. All were new in 1968/9 and the 'MB' type differed from the 'MBS' type in that they also had a lower driving position. This made them unpopular with drivers as it restricted their all round visibility and it also offered them less protection in the event of a front end collision. A total of 49 vehicles were acquired in four batches between March 1979 and May 1980.

The first four vehicles to arrive were allocated fleet Nos 2555–8 but these numbers were never carried. It was decided to allocate a new fleet number series to the ex London Country Merlins commencing at No 621. The first batch of fourteen vehicles arrived in March and April 1979 and was allocated fleet

Nos 621–34. The first three vehicles were the 45-seat 'MB' type, the remaining members of the batch being the 'MBS' type. May 1979 saw the arrival of a further ten vehicles which were allocated fleet Nos 635–44. Again the first three vehicles were of the 'MB' type, the remainder being the 'MBS' version. A further batch of thirteen vehicles arrived in August 1979, becoming fleet Nos 645–57, the first four being of the 'MB' type and the remainder 'MBS'. Of these three batches, Nos 622 (SMM 91F), 636 (VLW 93G), 638 (VLW 272G) and 642 (VLW 407G) were never operated by Citybus. The remainder were placed in traffic between May 1979 and April 1980. Number 655 (VLW 429G) was withdrawn in December 1980 following an accident and No 645 (VLW 102G) suffered the same fate in October 1981. A further eight became victims of the Troubles between November 1979 and July 1981. Normal withdrawals commenced in October 1980 with the final examples withdrawn in March 1982.

Although similar to the London Transport Merlins, these vehicles had not benefited from the London Transport maintenance regime where vehicles outshopped after major overhaul were virtually in 'as new' condition. Consequently many of the London Country Merlins were withdrawn after major mechanical or body failures. One final batch of twelve AEC Merlins was acquired from London Country in May 1980 – four of the 'MB' type and eight of the 'MBS' type. Although allocated fleet Nos 658–69, none of the batch was ever prepared for service and all were sold for scrap in 1981. The availability of more suitable and reliable vehicles had effectively sealed their fate.

Four more former London Transport AEC Merlins were acquired in May 1979. These however came from the fleet of Mid-Warwickshire Motors, Balsall Common who had acquired them from London Transport in January 1977. These were of the 50-seat single-door 'MB' type and were placed in service between May and July 1979 as fleet Nos 2551–4 following repaint and downseating to 49. Two were destroyed in a firebomb attack on Ardoyne depot in February 1980, the other two being withdrawn the following year.

A further two London Transport vehicles were acquired in August 1979 from Wombwell Diesels, Barnsley to provide spare parts for the rest of the fleet. VLW 77G was a MCW-bodied AEC Merlin and JGF 813K was a Metro Cammell-bodied AEC Swift. After stripping for parts, both were sold for scrap.

A solitary London Transport AEC Swift was transferred from the Ulsterbus fleet in December 1979. Number 15 (EGN 562J) had entered service with Citybus in May 1978, being transferred to Ulsterbus the following month to cover for heavy losses in the Londonderry City Services fleet. It was finally withdrawn in May 1980.

Following two disastrous firebomb attacks on Falls Park and Ardoyne depots in February 1980 which claimed a total of 40 vehicles, a batch of 15 vehicles was transferred in from the Ulsterbus fleet. Marshall-bodied former London Transport AEC Swift No 4 (EGN 206J) and Metro Cammell-bodied sisters Nos 13/7 (EGN 560/79J), 18 (EGN 608J) and 25 (EGN 594J) had originally been acquired by Citybus in 1978. They had subsequently been transferred to Ulsterbus to cover for heavy losses in the Londonderry City Services fleet. All were withdrawn in 1980, No 25 (EGN 594J) having been maliciously destroyed.

The fifteen also contained two unusual vehicles in the shape of 45-seat Bedford VAM14s with Duple Northern bodies, Nos 1218/59 (1218/59 TZ). Built primarily for rural work, their high floor line and narrow entrance, partially obstructed by the front mounted engine, made them somewhat unsuitable for city work. Both tended to be used for private hire work or as engineer's runabouts. Number 1218 met a premature end in July 1980 when it was destroyed in a further firebomb attack on Ardoyne depot. Number 1259 was withdrawn and scrapped later the same year.

The remaining eight vehicles were former London Transport AEC Merlins. Numbers 2490/7 (VLW 460G, AML 576H) were part of a batch of nine 'MBA' standee type vehicles purchased for the Citybus fleet in 1977. Heavy losses in the Ulsterbus fleet saw five of the nine transferred to Ulsterbus in March and April 1978 for use on Londonderry City Services. Number 2490 was maliciously destroyed in December 1980 whilst No 2497 was renumbered 670 in September 1981, being finally withdrawn two months later.

Throughout the 1970s the malicious destruction of vehicles continued and the company was always on the look out for good second-hand purchases. In 1980 Crosville Motor Services of Chester were able to supply 16 surplus Bristol REs, although with unfamiliar bodywork by Eastern Coach Works of Lowestoft. Number 710, in the hands of Driver Billy Elliman, is seen on the extension of the Greencastle service to the Abbey Centre. *Paul Savage*

Numbers 2511–3/7/8 (VLW 346/52/3/64/87G) and 2522 (VLW 366G) formed part of two batches of 'MB' type fully seated vehicles purchased for use by Ulsterbus between March and May 1977. Numbers 2512/3/8 and 2522 were all withdrawn in 1981, three having been maliciously destroyed. Numbers 2511/7 were renumbered 673/4 in October 1981, both being withdrawn in March 1982, No 674 having suffered malicious damage.

A further example of the 'MB' type AEC Merlins, No 2508 (VLW 370G), was acquired from Ulsterbus in May 1980. This vehicle lasted only six months before being withdrawn and scrapped.

1980 saw a major switch in policy with regard to the purchase of second-hand vehicles when in March a batch of 16 Bristol RELL6Gs were acquired from Crosville Motor Services, Chester. These vehicles dated from 1967/8 and were fitted with Eastern Coach Works 53-seat bus bodies. They were allocated fleet Nos 700–16 and arrived in three batches – Nos 701–6 in March, Nos 700/7–9/13/5 in April and Nos 710/1/2/4 in November. They were fitted with the twin shallow flat windscreens common on the early vehicles of this type. All were placed in service between April 1980 and January 1981 and proved to be both welcome and popular additions to the fleet. Of the initial batch of six, three initially had a cream surround to the destination display whilst the remaining three had the surround painted red. It was later decided that the red surround would become standard and the other three were quickly repainted to match. Of the batch No 702 was withdrawn in 1981 following an accident and between 1982 and 1988 a further 13 were to be destroyed as a result of the Troubles. Number 705 (SFM 22F) and No 706 (UFM 44F) survived in service until August 1989. Number 706 nearly made it into preservation. It was one of a number of vehicles to return to the mainland, being sold in August 1990 to United Provincial (t/a Pennine Blue), Dukinfield.

The second source of Eastern Coach Works-bodied Bristol REs was United Automobile Services of Darlington who supplied 17 between June 1980 and February 1981. Number 725 was the last of the batch to survive, being destroyed in 1988. Note the number of windows replaced with plain glass, the hopper/slider panes having been broken by stone throwing youths. This shot was taken in Castle Street, the traditional departure point for Falls Road services. *Paul Savage*

Whilst a commercial operation, the directors of the company were all heavily involved in bus preservation. Number 706 was intended for eventual restoration but when one of their active REs required an engine, it was removed from No 706 to get the other vehicle running again. Following the eventual collapse of this operation, the shell of No 706 was sold to a breaker.

Well pleased with these purchases, Citybus engineers were on the lookout for more examples to bolster the fleet. Crosville were unable to release any more vehicles at this time but another large operator of the type, United Automobile Services of Darlington, were able to supply a batch of 17. Allocated fleet Nos 716–32, they arrived in five batches between June 1980 and February 1981. These vehicles were new in 1968/9 and as with the previous batch, all had the flat two piece windscreen. The 1969 built examples (Nos 718/27–32) however had the later deeper two piece windscreen. Number 723 (THN 895F) suffered damage whilst in transit to Northern Ireland and was broken up for spare parts. Of the remainder No 732 (WHN 401G) was withdrawn in 1981 after a collision which also claimed former Crosville vehicle No 702 (OFM 14E). Of the surviving 15, the Troubles were to claim 12 between 1981 and 1983 and Nos 729/30 (YHN 804/6H) were withdrawn and scrapped in 1984. Sole survivor No 725 (THN 887F) survived until March 1988 when it was also destroyed.

A solitary example was acquired from Crosville in March 1984 and became fleet No 734 (UFM 46F). This vehicle was placed in service in June 1981 and operated the Royal Victoria Hospital outpatient's service until this service was discontinued in September 1983. It then returned to normal duties until it, too, was destroyed in May 1989.

Those of you paying attention will have noticed that there was no fleet No 733. Some of the 'older hands' working for the company tended to refer to the vehicles inherited from Belfast Corporation Transport by their original fleet numbers. As Potters-bodied Daimler Fleetline No 733 (733 UZ) was still current, albeit now numbered 2733, it was decided to leave fleet No 733 vacant to avoid any confusion.

Four second-hand REs were acquired in July 1981 from yet another new source, West Yorkshire Road Car of Harrogate. New in 1969, these vehicles had the deeper two piece flat windscreens. Allocated fleet Nos 735–8, three were destroyed between 1983 and 1987, sole survivor No 735 (BWU 552H) being withdrawn in October 1988 following an accident.

Crosville also supplied a further batch of six 1968/9-built REs in July 1981. The 1968 vehicles had the shallow flat windscreens whilst the two 1969 vehicles had the later deeper windscreens. Fleet Nos 739–44 were allocated and five were destroyed between 1982 and 1985, leaving just No 740 (UFM 43F) which was finally withdrawn in March 1989.

Delivery of new Bristol REs during 1981/2 resulted in the fleet numbers of several former London Transport AEC Merlins being duplicated with the new vehicles. In order to avoid this Merlins Nos 2497 (AML 576H), 2498 (VLW 451G), 2502 (AML 603H), 2511/7 (VLW 346/64G) and 2528 (VLW 222G) were renumbered 670–5 in September 1981, these fleet numbers following on from the former London Country AEC Merlins. They did not survive long in their new guise, two being withdrawn in October 1981 and a further two the following month. The remaining two vehicles survived until March 1982, one being withdrawn after suffering malicious damage. A further six Merlins were renumbered in April 1982 to once again release their former fleet numbers for new vehicles when Nos 2534/5 (WMT 619/20G) and 2536/45/8/9 (AML 625/52/9/61H) became Nos 676–81. This however was a paper exercise only, the vehicles having already been withdrawn and held in reserve. In the event none returned to traffic and all were sold in 1982/3. Number 678 (AML 625H) returned to England for preservation, the remainder, along with several others of the type, also returned to England but this time passing to Wombwell Diesels, Barnsley for breaking up. Ironically Wombwell Diesels had been a major breaker of London Transport buses for many years and Citybus had even acquired a number of AEC Merlins and Swifts from this source for spare parts for their own fleet of these vehicles.

It was to be two years before any further Bristol REs were acquired. Numbers 745–51 were new in 1971/2 and came from the fleet of West Riding Automobile Co, Wakefield. These were the first of the type to have the more attractive curved wrap around windscreens. All seven vehicles of this batch fell victim to the Troubles between 1984 and 1988, No 750 (AHL 233K) lasting a mere six days in service.

Between May and July 1983, a further batch of 13 vehicles was acquired from West Yorkshire Road Car. New between 1971 and 1973, all had the later curved windscreens. Given fleet Nos 752–64, the first five of the batch were allocated to the Ulsterbus fleet for use on Londonderry City Services. Of the eight allocated to the Citybus fleet, four were destroyed between 1984 and 1986, the remaining four surviving until the demise of the type in 1990.

In September 1983, a further three vehicles were acquired from the same source, but this time they were the shorter RESL6G model seating only 47. They were the first of the type to be purchased and were given fleet Nos 765–7. New in 1972, they all had curved windscreens. As Ulsterbus was experiencing a vehicle shortage at this time, all three were transferred to that company for use on Londonderry City Services.

United Automobile Services supplied a further batch of seven Bristol REs in October 1984. These dated from 1971/2 and had the later curved windscreens. Fleet Nos 768–74 were allocated and most of the batch was prepared for service then held in reserve, not finally entering service until 1985. Six were destroyed as a result of the Troubles, sole survivor No 772 (NHN 766K) lasting until the end of the type in 1990.

United Automobile Services supplied more Bristol REs in 1985 – eight standard length (36'0") RELLs and two shorter Bristol RESLs. RELL No 778 was caught by our photographer in a litter strewn Castle Street about to depart for Glen Road. Glen Road terminus at Glencolin was to see the last run by a Citybus Bristol RE, No 2548, on 31 January 2004.

Paul Savage

October 1984 also saw the arrival of two second-hand REs from yet another new source, East Midland Motor Services of Chesterfield. Dating from 1972, these vehicles had the later curved windscreen. They were unusual in that they were built with dual-door bodies but were subsequently rebuilt to single-door layout. Allocated fleet Nos 775/6, the latter lasted only four months before being destroyed. Number 775 (GVO 550K) remained in traffic until 1990.

A solitary example arrived from West Yorkshire Road Car in November 1984 as fleet No 777. This vehicle was new in 1973 and had the later curved windscreen. It was not placed in service until May 1985 and survived until March 1988 when it was destroyed.

One again it was United Automobile Services who supplied the next batch of vehicles – eight of the standard Bristol RELL6G with Eastern Coach Works 50-seat bodies and two of the shorter RESL6G which had 47-seat bodies. New in 1971/2, all had the more stylish curved windscreens. Allocated fleet Nos 778–87, two of the RELL6Gs (Nos 782/3) and the two RESL6Gs (Nos 786/7) were allocated to the Ulsterbus fleet for use on Londonderry City services. The remainder were prepared for service in 1985/6, finally entering service between 1985 and 1987. All six of the Citybus vehicles met a premature end, being destroyed between 1985 and 1988.

Another new source of vehicles was tapped in February 1985 when Eastern National Omnibus Co of Chelmsford supplied a batch of nine vehicles. They dated from 1970–2 and were of the curved windscreen variety. Becoming fleet Nos 788–96, four were once again allocated to the Ulsterbus fleet for use on Londonderry City services (Nos 788/9/95/6). The remaining five were placed in store, not being prepared for service until 1986/7. Placed in traffic in 1987, once again the entire batch were victims of the Troubles, being destroyed between 1987 and 1989.

Fleet number 714 was carried by three different second-hand Bristol REs. Perhaps the most unfortunate was freshly overhauled 'number two', a former Eastern National example, which was hijacked on its way from Falls Park to Ardoyne where it was to replace a vehicle destroyed earlier. This picture, taken at Ardoyne depot, is believed to be the only photograph of No 714(2) wearing Citybus red and ivory! *Mark O'Neill*

A further batch of five vehicles arrived from United Automobile Services in November 1985. All dated from 1982 and had the later style of ECW bodywork. Four were given fleet Nos 797–800 at which point Citybus ran out of fleet numbers, No 801 upwards being allocated to the Ulsterbus minibus fleet. By now there were quite a number of gaps in the 7xx fleet number series due to the withdrawal of earlier acquisitions, most of which had been destroyed in the Troubles. It was decided to re-use fleet numbers of already withdrawn vehicles and consequently the fifth vehicle of this batch became the second No 702. Vehicles in the fleet listings with re-used fleet numbers have a (2) after their fleet numbers and in one instance there is even a (3)! Finally placed in traffic in 1986/7, this batch had particularly short lives, four being destroyed in 1987 and the remaining example in 1989.

In April 1986, the remaining 11 REs in the fleet of Eastern National were acquired, Dating from 1971/2, all had the later curved windscreens. They became Citybus fleet Nos 704/7/9–15/7/8(2) and were initially stored before being placed in service in 1987. All bar one of these vehicles was destroyed between 1987 and 1989 and one never even made it into traffic. Number 714(2) (WNO 538L) had been overhauled and freshly repainted and had just passed PSV. It was on its way to Ardoyne depot to take up duty, replacing another vehicle which had been destroyed earlier in the day, when it was also seized and set on fire. The solitary survivor of the batch, No 717(2) (WNO 542L), was withdrawn in 1989.

In an effort to provide vehicles more suitable for undertaking tours and private hire work, two Leyland Leopard PSU3E/4R with Plaxton Supreme 53-seat coach bodies were transferred from the Ulsterbus fleet in April 1987. Numbers 561/2 (XOI 561/2) continued to perform these duties until returned to Ulsterbus in 1992, having been replaced by newer vehicles.

Up until this point Citybus had tried to concentrate on obtaining what was basically a standard vehicle, the single-door Eastern Coach Works-bodied Gardner engined Bristol RE. Where the shorter RESL6G

Citybus really didn't have any vehicles suitable for long distance private hires or tours so in an attempt to remedy this situation two Plaxton Supreme IV-bodied Leyland Leopards, Nos 561/2, were transferred from Ulsterbus Tours in April 1987. They retained the same style of livery application, albeit with the blue painted red. Number 562 is seen at the Manor House, Ulster Folk & Transport Museum, Cultra, Co Down. *Paul Savage*

model had been acquired, the running units at least were compatible with their bigger brothers. By 1987 the Bristol RE had largely been eliminated from the National Bus Company fleets and it was becoming increasingly difficult to obtain batches of the 'standard' vehicle. As time went by, Citybus were forced to pick up what they could get, including dual-door examples and a number with the nonstandard Leyland 680 engine. From an engineering point of view, this was probably a major headache but from the enthusiast's point of view, it added more interest to the fleet.

The first 'nonstandard' vehicles to arrive were a batch of five Bristol RESL6Ls acquired from Ribble Motor Services, Preston in April 1986. All were new in 1971 and had the later style body, with curved windscreens. In addition to being the shorter model, they were powered by the Leyland 680 engine and were the first second-hand purchases to be equipped with the Leyland unit. Allocated fleet Nos 719–23(2), it was decided to transfer all five to the Ulsterbus fleet who already had considerable experience with the 680 engine in both the original batch of Bristol REs and in the Leyland Leopard. All were placed in service in late 1986 on Londonderry City Services.

Crosville supplied a further two REs in June 1987 but these had 48-seat dual-door bodies, the first second-hand dual-door bodies to be taken into stock. As fleet Nos 703/8(2), both were initially prepared for service and then stored, not entering service until late 1987. Both were withdrawn in 1989, No 708(2) (HFM 199J) having been hijacked and destroyed.

A solitary RE was acquired from Wilts & Dorset Bus Co, Poole in June 1987. Dating from 1981, it was a standard RELL6G with curved windscreens, but was fitted with 50 coach type seats. This vehicle was given fleet number 714, the third such vehicle to carry this number. It was prepared for service but then stored until March 1988 before being placed in traffic. As the nonstandard seating would be particularly prone to vandalism, it tended to be confined to private hire work with only occasional sorties out into normal service. It was withdrawn from traffic in March 1989 and was converted to a driver-training vehicle, a role it was to fulfil until withdrawn and scrapped in August 1990.

In June 1987 two slightly unusual Bristol REs were acquired. Latterly in the fleet of United Counties Omnibus Co, Northampton, this pair was acquired via a mainland dealer. New in 1968, these vehicles were of the flat windscreens but both had an unusual 'T' shaped destination display, the first and only examples in the fleet. Allocated fleet Nos 716(2)/24(2), both were prepared for service and then stored, No 716(2) (RBD 330G) entering traffic in December 1987 and No 724(2) (RBD 319G) in March the following year. Number 716(2) was a further victim of the Troubles, being hijacked and destroyed in May 1989. Number 724(2) survived in service until April 1980, returning to the mainland for preservation two months later.

The final four vehicles to be acquired from Crosville were received in July 1987. Three were dual-door Bristol RELL6G similar to Nos 703/8(2) acquired the previous month. Fleet Nos 726–8(2) were allocated and all were prepared for service, then stored, not seeing use until March 1988. Number 726(2) (HFM 190J) was destroyed in August 1989, the other two being finally withdrawn in January 1990. Number 728(2) (HFM 196J) later returned to the mainland for preservation. The fourth vehicle in the batch was one of the shorter RESL6G models with Eastern Coach Works 46-seat body. New in 1968, this vehicle had the shallow, flat windscreen style of bodywork Allocated fleet No 729(2), it was not placed in service until March 1988. Sadly its service life was to be a brief one as it was hijacked and destroyed in west Belfast in August 1988.

In August 1987 Cumberland Motor Services of Whitehaven supplied Citybus with nine dual-door Eastern Coach Works-bodied, Leyland-engined Bristol RELLs which had been in use on contract work at the Sellafield nuclear plant. Once it became known where these vehicles had originated rumours began to circulate that they were lead-lined and glowed in the dark! Number 731(2), in National Bus Company green, with red on white **CITYBUS** fleetnames, waits time in Donegall Place, outside the much missed Anderson & McAuley department store, before heading for Shaw's Road on service 15.

Paul Savage

Another new source for vehicles was found in August 1987 when a batch of nine was acquired from Cumberland Motor Services, Whitehaven. These vehicles brought yet more variety to the fleet in that not only were they dual-door vehicles but they were also powered by the Leyland 680 engine in place of the Gardner unit favoured by Citybus up to this point. These vehicles had been new to Bristol Omnibus but had been acquired by Cumberland to operate a contract service at the Sellafield nuclear plant in Cumbria. Fleet Nos 730–2/9/41–4/6(2) were allocated to the batch and such was the shortage of vehicles at this time that Nos 730/1/9/41/2(2) were placed in service still in National Bus Company leaf green, with Citybus fleetnames applied. Numbers 730(2) and 742(2) did not survive long enough to be repainted into Citybus livery, both being destroyed in August 1988. Over their short lives in the Citybus fleet, a number of 'urban myths' originated concerning these vehicles. Because of their association with Sellafield, rumours starting circulating that these vehicles had bodies lined with lead to prevent the passage of radiation and it was also rumoured that they "glowed in the dark". A further two of the batch were destroyed in 1989, the remainder being withdrawn in 1989/90. Three of the batch returned to the mainland for further use and at least one subsequently passed into preservation.

Three further Leyland engined examples arrived in August 1987, but this time from Ribble Motor Services, Preston. New in 1971/2, all were of the shorter RESL6L type and all had curved windscreens. Allocated fleet Nos 733/6/8(2), all were prepared for service and then stored, finally entering service in 1988/9. Number 736(2) (OCK 347K) was destroyed in August 1989 and No 733(2) (OCK 342K) was withdrawn the following month after suffering accident damage. The sole survivor was withdrawn in 1990 and returned to the mainland for possible future use.

Crosville Wales, based at Llandudno, supplied a batch of four Bristol RELL6G in September 1987. All were new in 1970 and had 53-seat single-door bodies and the later curved windscreens. Given fleet Nos 747–50(2), all were prepared for service in 1987/8, finally entering service in 1988/9. Number 750(2) (HFM 208J) was the first of the batch to be withdrawn, being destroyed in July 1989. Of the remainder, both Nos 747(2) (EFM 178H) and 748(2) (EFM 181H) returned to the mainland on withdrawal, No 747 for further use and No 748(2) for preservation.

One benefit of having standard service type vehicles in both the Citybus and Ulsterbus fleets was that it was possible to transfer them between fleets. In 1987 Ulsterbus found themselves in the position of having a number of surplus Alexander-bodied Bristol REs. Between September and December a total of nine were transferred to the Citybus fleet – Nos 2232 (ROI 2232), 2276/87/9 (TOI 2276/87/9), 2301 (TOI 2301), 2363 (UOI 2363), 2442/53 (WOI 2442/53) and 2591 (BXI 2591). These were overhauled at the Falls Park workshops before being placed in traffic. The only major change, apart from repainting, was the replacement of the nearside front double back to back seat over the wheelarch with a triple bench seat, thus reducing the seating capacity from 52 to 51. Number 2289 was destroyed in February 1991 and No 2363 was withdrawn following an accident in October 1995. Number 2442 was withdrawn and scrapped in 1996 after suffering a major chassis failure. On withdrawal by Citybus, the remainder returned to the Ulsterbus fleet for further use. The transfer of these vehicles from Ulsterbus was the beginning of the end for the second-hand RE fleet. It was a cheaper option to having to carry out major overhauls on vehicles that were often in poor condition and in some cases nonstandard.

Between January and November 1988, a further 14 Alexander-bodied REs were transferred from the Ulsterbus fleet – Nos 2173/9 (POI 2173/9), 2241/2/6/7/61 (ROI 2241/2/6/7/61), 2288/96/7/9 (TOI 2288/96/7/9), 2361/2 (UOI 2361/2) and 2433 (WOI 2433). As with the previous batch, all were downseated to 51. Number 2261 was unusual in that it was one of two Ulsterbus examples rebodied in 1983 after their original bodies had been destroyed in malicious fires. Numbers 2241/7/61 and 2296 all met premature ends, being destroyed between 1989 and 1992. Number 2288 was withdrawn in April 1992 after suffering accident damage. The body on this vehicle was scrapped and the chassis was cosmetically restored and is now on display at the Bristol Science Museum. Numbers 2173/9 were withdrawn in 1991 and subsequently formed part of a sizeable batch sold to Bus Eireann in Dublin for use as school buses, becoming their 'BG class'. Apart from No 2361, which was withdrawn and scrapped in 1995, the remainder returned to Ulsterbus for further use on withdrawal.

By 1988 United Automobile Services had withdrawn the last of the longer Bristol RELL6G model but were still in a position to supply eight of the shorter RESL6G model. Dating from 1971/2, all had the later curved windscreens. Acquired in March 1988, these vehicles were in relatively poor condition and all were placed in store. Allocated fleet Nos 751–4/6/7/9/60(2), by now the need for second-hand vehicles was diminishing and in the event only the first three were prepared for service, finally entering service in 1989. The remaining five remained in secure storage before being sold for scrap in 1990/1. Number 752(2) (JHN 565K) was destroyed in October 1989 after only two months in service and No 751(2) (JHN 566K) lasted only three weeks before being withdrawn after a major mechanical failure. Number 753(2) (JHN 561K) was finally withdrawn in September 1990, returning to the mainland in 1991 for further use.

Five more Leyland-engined Bristol RESL6Ls were acquired from Ribble Motor Services in April 1988. Allocated fleet Nos 764–8(2), they dated from 1971/2 and had the curved windscreens. All five were prepared for service but only four actually entered traffic, No 767(2) (OCK 359K) being sold to a local school without being used. Due to vehicle shortages Nos 764(2) (NCK 338J) and 766(2) (OCK 350K) were placed in traffic in Ribble livery with Citybus fleetnames applied. Both were taken out of service early in 1989, returning to service later in the year in full Citybus colours. All were withdrawn in 1990 and Nos 764(2) (NCK 338J) and 766(2) (OCK 350K) subsequently returned to the mainland for further use, both eventually passing into preservation.

In May 1988 a mixed batch of four of the shorter Bristol REs was acquired from Yelloway Motor Services, Rochdale. Numbers 769/73(2) (LTG 35/41L) were Leyland engined examples and had 44-seat single-door bodies with curved windscreens. New to Welsh municipal operator Aberdare in 1972, both were prepared for service in 1988 and finally entered service in August of the following year. Both had short lives, being withdrawn by the end of 1989 and both subsequently returned to the mainland for further use. Number 770(2) (JEH 187K) was also Leyland powered and also had a 44-seat body with curved windscreens. It was new in 1971 to Potteries Motor Traction, Stoke on Trent. It was prepared for service in 1988, finally entering service in August 1989. It was withdrawn at the end of the same month after only three weeks use and was sold for scrap in 1991. The final vehicle of the quartet, No 771(2) (NHB 188M), was new in 1973 and was Gardner engined. It had a 47-seat body with curved windscreens. Like Nos 769/73(2), it was also new to a Welsh municipal operator but this time Merthyr Tydfil. Prepared for service in 1988, it also entered service in August 1989 and, like No 770(2), was withdrawn after only three weeks. It was sold in 1991 for further use on the mainland.

A further two Ribble Motor Services Bristol RESL6Ls were acquired in July 1988 via a mainland dealer. Dating from 1971/2, both were in relatively poor condition and were placed in store. Although allocated fleet Nos 774/6(2), neither was prepared for service and both were eventually sold for scrap in 1990.

In September 1988, three Bristol RELL6Gs were acquired from Cambus, Cambridge. All dated from 1970 and had been new to Eastern Counties Omnibus Company. Allocated fleet Nos 777–9(2), No 777(2) (YNG 725J) had 53 bus seats and the later curved windscreens. Numbers 778(2) (WNG 864H) and 779(2) (XAH 873H) had 50 coach type seats and the deeper flat windscreens. All were prepared for service in 1988, No 777(2) finally entering service in 1989. Because of their coach seating, the other two were not used in passenger service, becoming driver-training vehicles in April 1989. All were withdrawn in 1990 and subsequently returned to the mainland, No 778(2) for preservation and Nos 777/9(2) for possible further use.

Two further Bristol RELL6Gs were acquired in November 1988, this time from West Sussex County Council, who had been using them as school buses. Originally five were expected but in the event only two turned up. New in 1972 to Trent Motor Traction in Stoke on Trent, both were in poor condition. Although allocated fleet Nos 780/2(2), neither was prepared for service and both were eventually sold for scrap in 1990.

Also acquired the same month was a solitary vehicle from private operator, Kettlewell of Retford. The reason this vehicle was purchased is something of a mystery as it was nonstandard in a number of aspects. New in 1972 to Bristol Omnibus, this vehicle was a Bristol RELH6L with Eastern Coach Works body fitted with 49 coach seats. The RELH chassis was a high frame version of the RE and was used primarily for vehicles used on long distance rural and motorway type work. Besides the higher floor line, the other main difference was the absence of the rear emergency door standard on the RESL/RELL model, a full width rear window being fitted instead. This vehicle became fleet No 785(2) and although prepared for service, it was not used. As with the other coach-seated examples, it became a driver trainer in April 1989. It was withdrawn in 1990 and returned to the mainland for further use.

The final Bristol RELL6G to be acquired arrived in December 1988. Allocated fleet No 786(2), it was new in 1971 to Western National and had the curved windscreen style of body. It was acquired from Cumberland Motor Services Ltd, Whitehaven who had obtained it with the fleet and operations of a private operator. It was not prepared for service and returned to the mainland in 1991 for further use.

By late 1988 Ulsterbus no longer had any requirement for the few survivors of their fleet of second-hand Bristol REs and the four remaining vehicles were transferred to Citybus in November. Three of the vehicles to return were Leyland engined Bristol RESL6Ls which had been new to Ribble – Nos 721(2) (NCK 331J), 722(2) (NCK 335J) and 723(2) (NCK 334J). Of these No 723(2) was already out of service with an

Ribble Motor Services of Preston, who had previously supplied Ulsterbus with a number of Leyland Leopard buses, sold five Leyland-engined Bristol RESLs to Citybus in April 1988. Here, in Donegall Square North, No 764(2) waits time before heading north to Cavehill Road and Carr's Glen. Number 764(2) is now preserved in England and has been restored to Ribble colours in 'as delivered' condition (see page 152). *Paul Savage*

engine defect and never operated for Citybus, being used instead as a source of spare parts. The other vehicle to return was the sole survivor of the four former Eastern National vehicles allocated to Ulsterbus, No 789 (MHK 914J). None of these vehicles had been fitted with destination displays whilst operating in Londonderry and some even had the destination gear removed. On some the destination glass had been broken and rather than replace it, the destination display was panelled over. As a result they could not be used in normal service and were confined to schools duties. All retained Ulsterbus livery during their short stay with Citybus. They were withdrawn in 1989 and subsequently scrapped.

Although strictly outside the period covered by this book, the final batch of second-hand Bristol REs to be acquired were a further batch of eight Bristol RESL6Ls which were purchased in January/February 1989. These came from the fleet of North Western Road Car Co Ltd of Bottle but had been new to Ribble Motor Services, Preston and were similar to the previous batches of vehicles from this source. All dated from 1971/2 and had curved windscreens. Fleet Nos 781/3/4/7/8/90–2(2) were allocated but in the event only Nos 787(2) (OCK 344K) and 788(2) (OCK 358K) were prepared for use. Both finally entered service in August 1989, No 787(2) being withdrawn after only three weeks. Number 788(2) fared little better and was withdrawn in January 1990. The remaining six were kept in store, being sold in 1990/1. Six of the batch of eight returned to England for further use, but all were subsequently scrapped.

Number 786(2), on the left of the picture, was the last Bristol RELL to be acquired although eight RESLs, including No 787(2) were purchased from North Western Road Car of Bootle in January/February 1989. Number 786(2) was supplied by Cumberland Motor Services who had acquired it with the operations of Yeowarts of Whitehaven. It had been new to Western National of Plymouth.

Paul Savage

Helping Hands

As well as the second-hand additions, from time to time a number of vehicles were borrowed from Ulsterbus to bolster the fleet. Serious vehicle shortages in 1975 saw a total of 14 Leyland Leopards borrowed from Ulsterbus between February and May. These were Nos 1301/6/8/10/5/8/21/2/4/6/7/31/2 (4001/6/8/10 /5/8/21/2/4/6/7/31/2 WZ) and 1375 (BOI 1375). Numbers 1301/6/8/10/5/8 had 53-seat bus bodies built by Potters, the forerunner of Alexander (Belfast) while numbers 1321/2/6/7/31/2 also had Potters bodies, but this time with 49 dual-purpose seats. Number 1375 (BOI 1375) also had a 49-seat dual-purpose body but this time by Alexander (Belfast). The one remaining vehicle, No 1324 (4024 WZ), also had an Alexander (Belfast) body but with 53 bus seats. This vehicle originally had been fitted with a Potters body but was rebodied in March 1973 after its original body had been maliciously destroyed in July of the previous year. All retained Ulsterbus livery but with the addition of Citybus fleetnames to the front and sides. In order to allow the fitting of ticket equipment, one double nearside seat was removed. The high floor line of these vehicles made them unsuitable for city service work and so they tended to be confined to schools services and private hire work although occasional forays into normal service were made. All returned to Ulsterbus in November 1975 with the exception of Nos 1326/7 (4026/7 WZ) which were retained until January 1976.

In May 1976 Ulsterbus loaned Alexander (Belfast)-bodied Leyland Atlantean No 947 (COI 947) to Citybus. This vehicle carried an allover advertising livery for Sealink who were keen that their advert should gain some exposure in the Greater Belfast area. To replace it at Craigavon, Citybus loaned rebodied Daimler Fleetline/Alexander (Belfast) No 2857 (EOI 4857). This vehicle did not prove popular with Craigavon crews and at the end of June 1976, it was replaced by Leyland Atlantean/Alexander (Belfast) No 2911 (JOI 2911). This vehicle remained at Craigavon until September 1976 when No 947 returned home.

Over the years vehicles were transferred between the two fleets to cover for vehicles maliciously destroyed, or when occasional short-term increases in vehicle requirements existed. In May 1976 Ulsterbus Leyland Atlantean No 947, which was based at Craigavon and carried an allover advert for Sealink's Larne–Stranraer route, was transferred to Short Strand so that the advert would be more widely seen. In this view in Donegall Square West the driver's 'Ultimate' ticket machine and the yellow 'M' token machine can just be seen through the windscreen.
Raymond Bell

Heavy losses in early 1980 saw four unusual additions to the fleet. In February UTA-bodied Leyland Tiger Cub No 454 (7454 CZ) was received on loan. Again it retained Ulsterbus livery with the addition of Citybus fleetnames to the front and sides. It was returned to Ulsterbus in mid March, having spent most of its time on school duties. Also received during February were three Marshall-bodied Leyland Leopards, Nos 1142/5/6 (CRN 819/24/7D). These vehicles were part of a batch of ten which Ulsterbus had acquired from Ribble Motor Services, Preston in July 1979. Again these vehicles retained Ulsterbus livery with the addition of Citybus fleetnames. All three were used on the Citylink service linking Central and York Road railway stations via Belfast City Centre. They remained on this operation until April 1980 when they were returned to Ulsterbus.

In May 1984 an Alexander-bodied Leyland Atlantean was borrowed from Ulsterbus to provide a high capacity vehicle for private hire work. Number 955 (MDS 668P) was one of a number acquired from Strathclyde PTE in Glasgow between 1982 and 1984 for use on schools services. It remained with Citybus until September.

In addition to the official loans recorded in company records, many unofficial loans have taken place over the years, usually following major depot fires. These normally lasted only a few days until alternative arrangements could be made. On occasions brand new Ulsterbus vehicles awaiting delivery at the Alexander (Belfast) plant were drafted in for a few days to assist. Such vehicles were generally confined to schools and special workings in addition to private hire work where ticketing equipment was not required.

Loans from Citybus to Ulsterbus were much less common and generally only involved vehicles in allover advertising liveries. In April 1985 Bristol RE/Alexander (Belfast) No 2531 (AXI 2531), which carried an allover advert for the Youth Employment Service, was loaned to Ulsterbus being replaced in March 1986 by sister vehicle No 2541 (AXI 2541) which carried an updated advert for the same customer. This vehicle finally returned to Citybus in September 1987. A further vehicle from the same batch, No 2560 (AXI 2560) was loaned to Ulsterbus from August 1985 to April 1987. This vehicle carried an allover advert for the Coal Advisory Service. It returned to Ulsterbus once more in February 1988 for use on Londonderry City Services. It remained there until August 1989 when it was hijacked and destroyed while operating on one of the city routes. Perhaps the advert was a foretaste of things to come!

In May 1978 three of the Potters-bodied AEC Swifts, Nos 2766/7/71 (766/7/71 UZ), were loaned to Ulsterbus for use at a fishing festival in Enniskillen. Number 2771 was withdrawn at the end of May 1978 and was never to run again. It was moved to Londonderry to provide spare parts for the ex London Transport AEC Merlins and Swifts before being sold for scrap. Numbers 2766/7 remained with Ulsterbus until the end of August 1978 when both were returned to Citybus, No 2766 as a driver training vehicle and No 2767 being placed in the Reserve fleet.

November 1981 saw two double-deckers loaned to Ulsterbus for use on school services. Number 2733 (733 UZ), the sole surviving Potters-bodied Daimler Fleetline, was allocated to Coleraine. It remained there until February 1982 when it was involved in an accident. It was returned to Citybus the following month but was immediately withdrawn. The second vehicle was dual door Alexander (Belfast)-bodied Daimler Fleetline No 2872 (EOI 4872). Allocated to Omagh, it was returned to Citybus at the end of March 1982.

Four of the former Crosville ECW-bodied Bristol REs – Nos 705 (SFM 22F), 710 (OFM 15E) and 711/4 (SFM 17/20F) – were loaned to Ulsterbus in May 1984 to provide additional capacity for the Enniskillen fishing festival. Numbers 705/14 had returned to Citybus by the end of the month but Nos 710/1 were not returned until the end of June.

The inherited fleet

The situation which prevailed in the city from the late 1960s gave the remaining half cab double-deckers an extended lease of life, with the last Guy Arab IIIs surviving until 27 April 1975. In this view at Short Strand depot No 2344 leads a line-up of nine Guys one Sunday morning over 30 years ago. These buses gave 25 years service to the city of Belfast. Just visible above the fleet number is the depot allocation, something which disappeared fairly quickly from Citybus vehicles but which still features on Ulsterbus vehicles. Number 2346 survives in preservation, owned by the photographer. It is hoped that it will re-appear in 2005 after a major 'overhaul'.

Raymond Bell

Above: The other half cab buses in the fleet were Daimler CVG6s like No 2392 seen here parked up at Falls Park depot. The CVGs were the first 8'0" wide double-deckers delivered to the Corporation and the last of them, Nos 2389 and 2446, were withdrawn in October 1975, six months after the last of the Guys. Number 2446 was purchased for preservation and is currently in storage pending restoration work. *Raymond Bell*

Opposite top: Whilst we would have preferred to have pictures of these vehicles actually in service we have had difficulty locating suitable pictures, probably because wandering around the city with a camera wasn't necessarily the safest thing to be doing in the early 1970s. In this line-up at Falls Park depot we see four CVGs, led by No 2428. Alongside is Daimler Roadliner No 1298, one of two acquired by Ulsterbus with the business of Coastal Bus Service Ltd of Portrush. Unlike its sister No 1299, No 1298 wasn't used, other than as a source of spare parts. *Raymond Bell*

Opposite bottom: Number 2551 was an Alexander-bodied Leyland Atlantean which had been delivered to Belfast Corporation in 1960. It was never a successful bus and spent its last years in Belfast working from Short Strand depot on the special service operated for out-patients at the Royal Victoria Hospital. It is seen here parked up outside the workshop facility at Short Strand. *Raymond Bell*

Opposite top: The last of the MH Coachworks-bodied Daimler Fleetlines to remain in service was No 2600. Its final duty was a 'Farewell Tour' organised by the Irish Transport Trust, which visited various terminii around the city. Number 2600 is seen here in Donegall Square North heading to pick up the tour participants. The driver on that day was Peter Fusco (see photograph page 133).
Paul Savage

Opposite bottom: Taken minutes after the photograph directly above Fleetline No 2600 rests in Donegall Square South before starting out on its final job. Trolleybus traction poles are still much in evidence and carry the decorative lighting which surrounded the City Hall. In the distance, to the left of No 2600, the spire of Church House, the headquarters of the Presbyterian Church in Ireland, can just be glimpsed.
Paul Savage

Above: The 76 route to Gilnahirk had long been the preserve of 7'6" wide buses, mainly due to tight clearances through Cherryvalley. When the last of the Guys were withdrawn the route became Fleetline-operated (8'0" wide vehicles) and No 2605 is pictured here in the Shandon Park/Kensington Road area heading for Gilnahirk, having been diverted from its normal route. (Buses usually ran along this road in the opposite direction on the return journey from Gilnahirk.) Points of interest are the advert for the 'confidential telephone' and, as mentioned in the caption to the photograph on page 30, the painted yellow line indicating the floor level.
Raymond Bell

Opposite: MH Coachworks-bodied Daimler Fleetline No 2703 was displayed at the Commercial Motor Show at Earl's Court in 1964 and carried this livery variation, with red around the front upper deck windows, during its entire service life. In this picture it is seen in Upper Queen Street awaiting departure time for a run to Oldpark, which would take it past Ardoyne depot en route. Number 2703 was one of a number of vehicles fitted with an illuminated advertising panel on the offside.
Raymond Bell

Above: The evening sun catches Potter-bodied Daimler Fleetline No 2722 as it's parked up at Ardoyne depot at the end of its day's duty. Note the 'PAY ON ENTRY' board fitted on the front. This board was hinged so that it could be folded down if the the vehicle was being operated with a conductor on board. These boards were removed when conductor operation finally ceased.
Ian Houston

Opposite: In 1964 the Corporation purchased three Leyland Atlanteans with MH Coachworks bodies. They were numbered 704–6 and worked from Ardoyne, where No 706, as Citybus 2706, is seen. These vehicles were neither popular nor successful and spent much time off the road. All three were later transferred to Ulsterbus, for use on schools services, and they weren't much more reliable there!
Raymond Bell

59

Potter-bodied Daimler Fleetline No 2733 was one of six which were fitted with an air-operated gear change as opposed to the usual electric one. It was working on service 80 (Oldpark) when caught by the photographer at Alliance Avenue, in the north of the city. Number 2703 (previous page) was photographed at the city centre end of this route. Note the damage to No 2733's the roof, above the first window bay.

Paul Savage

Photographs of the Potter-bodied Daimler Roadliners in service with Citybus have proved almost impossible to obtain so I've chosen this shot of Nos 2749 and 2742 parked up at Falls Park to illustrate these unreliable vehicles; they probably spent quite a bit of time parked here in any circumstance!

Raymond Bell

In 2005 it would be difficult to find the exact spot where the upper picture was taken as the whole area has been redeveloped as part of the Lanyon Place scheme. AEC Swift No 2755 is parked on Laganbank Road, to the rear of Oxford Street Bus Station, just beside the River Lagan. Number 2755 was new in 1968 and was withdrawn in 1977. Number 2771 (below) was one of a number fitted with Darvic plastic panels as an experiment; it wasn't a success as the panels rippled in warm weather. Note the temporary repair to the nearside rear window.

Raymond Bell (above)/Author (below)

Opposite: Daimler Fleetline No 2803 waits time in Donegall Square West before working an evening journey out along the Antrim Road to Ballyhenry. As mentioned in the main text, youths throwing stones at buses is a problem in particular areas of Belfast. Apart from the obvious dangers No 2803 clearly illustrates another potential problem – a lack of ventilation when the sliding vents are replaced with plain glass. There are no opening windows on this side of the top deck. Number 2803 was also one of ten dual-door Fleetlines fitted with panels for illuminated advertising. *Paul Savage*

Above: Upper Queen Street is the location for this picture of Daimler Fleetline single-decker No 2780. The Alexander bodies on these vehicles gave great problems due to flexing of the chassis; a kink is clearly visible in the roof line just above the third window bay. Another point to note is that the destination and via blinds have been fitted in the wrong apertures, also the use of Castle Junction as the city centre terminus even though the vehicle would never reach there!
Paul Savage

Opposite: Looking north into Royal Avenue we see Fleetline No 2847 arriving in from Ballyhenry and Glengormley and heading through Castle Junction toward its terminus in Donegall Square West. These 33'0'" long vehicles, disliked by drivers for having heavy steering, featured a nearside staircase, the blank panel between the doors indicating its position. Royal Avenue has changed much since this photograph was taken. The bank on the left of the picture is now a Tesco store and the Avenue cinema, in the middle distance has disappeared under the Castle Court shopping development. An Ulsterbus Bristol RE working in on a Shore Road service can be seen on the right. *Paul Savage*

Opposite: Try doing this in 2005 and the Police Service of Northern Ireland might have something to say to you! One of the last vehicles delivered to the Corporation Transport Department was Alexander-bodied Daimler Fleetline No 854, seen here in Great Victoria Street as Citybus No 2854. This picture was taken on the last day of two-way traffic in this part of Great Victoria Street. Buildings of note are the Royal Naval Association club, to the left and the Spence Bryson carpet factory in the centre background. To the right of the picture the tower of the Technical College can just be seen.
Paul Savage

Above: We move out to Newtownabbey now with a view of Fleetline No 2862 turning out of the Carnmoney Road on its way to Mossley. The run from Glengormley village through to this point could prove a struggle in these Fleetlines. One of the differences between the AOI and EOI-registered buses was the headlamp arrangement. The AOI batch featured twin headlights and a single fog lamp whereas the EOI batch had single headlights and two fog lamps, although No 2862 seems to have lost one at some stage.
Paul Savage

Opposite: To promote the availability of advertising space on its buses numerous vehicles carried pictures of fruit and vegetables, such as the cucumbers seen here on Fleetline No 2856 waiting in Wellington Place before heading for Carr's Glen via Oldpark Road. Number 2856 would have worked into town from either Ormeau (ser 83) or Mount Merrion (ser 85) via Botanic Avenue and Great Victoria Street.
Ian Houston

Early acquisitions and loans

Above: In 1967 an AEC Swift was demonstrated to Ulsterbus. It was subsequently sold by AEC to Antrim County Council, which used it as a staff bus but after the second of two serious accidents, it was sold to Coastal who subsequently repaired it and placed it in service as their fleet No 6. On the takeover of Coastal by Ulsterbus Ltd, this vehicle was allocated to Londonderry for use on the city services, as No 1300, but was withdrawn at the end of June 1974. After a period in store it was transferred to the Citybus fleet in September 1975. *Raymond Bell*

Opposite: In 1975 Citybus borrowed 14 Leyland Leopards from Ulsterbus. Number 1324 (4024 WZ), seen at the turning circle at Ormeau, just opposite where Forestside shopping centre is today, carried an Alexander (Belfast) body with 53 bus seats. This vehicle had been fitted with a Potter body when new but was rebodied in March 1973 after its original body had been maliciously destroyed in July 1972. The Leopards retained Ulsterbus livery during their stay in the city but with the addition of 'Citybus' fleetnames to the front and sides. *Raymond Bell*

To help overcome vehicle shortages Citybus acquired a number of these Weymann-bodied Leyland Tiger Cubs from Ulsterbus in 1974/5. Number 1012 is seen here in Short Strand depot, in company with several others. *Raymond Bell*

New vehicles

Above: The first new vehicles delivered to Citybus were five Alexander-bodied Daimler Fleetlines – Nos 2863/5/70/1/2 – outstanding from a batch ordered by Belfast Corporation. This is No 2865 and the location is Donegall Square West. The bus is operating a service to Dundonald via Bloomfield, although you'd be hard pressed to know that given the information on the front of the bus! Rumour has it that the destination and via blinds had been fitted upside down.

Paul Savage

Opposite: The first new vehicles ordered for Citybus were 40 Leyland Atlanteans, which were bodied by Alexander's at Mallusk. All forty were allocated to Ardoyne but the whole batch never saw service together as No 2908 was hijacked and destroyed in February 1976 after only three weeks in service. This is No 2877, which wore this yellow-based allover advert for BEL-1, a local furniture retailer, from September 1979 to June 1984, when it was withdrawn. It was caught here at Mossley, in Newtownabbey.

Raymond Bell

The last vehicle in the batch was No 2872 which is seen here running down University Avenue en route to Mount Merrion. Part of the destination display has been panelled in and a Bristol style destination blind fitted in the 'via' box. This road still sees regular operation by double-deck vehicles on the Quality Bus Corridor to Four Winds.
Raymond Bell

Opposite: With their high capacity, and reasonable turn of speed, the Atlanteans were useful vehicles for private hires, such as Sunday school excursions and, as seen, here Loyal Order demonstrations. Leading this line of Atlanteans and Fleetlines in North Queen Street is Atlantean No 2893, which later became an open-top vehicle, replacing former Citybus Daimler Fleetline No 2716 on the Coleraine to the Giant's Causeway run. Number 2893 is parked outside Jennymount Methodist Church, which having burnt down several years previously was rebuilt and re-opened in 2004.

Raymond Bell

Above: Atlantean No 2884 was repainted in a variation of the standard livery with a deeper red section on the between decks panels after carrying a white-based wrap round advert for the Ulster Cancer Foundation; some of the white can still be seen. The scheme looked particularly odd at the front where the red came right down to the top of the windscreen. Compare No 2884 with Nos 2893 and 2907 opposite.

Raymond Bell

Opposite: Number 2907, seen here at Balmoral terminus, was another oddity. The previous double-deckers, the Alexander-bodied Daimler Fleetines, had been built with rubber gasket-mounted glazing but the Atlanteans reverted to the style where the glazing was fitted in pans. The nearside upper deck of No 2907 was damaged in a contretemps with a tree, resulting in a rebuild having to be undertaken. This was done using Fleetline parts and gave the unusual situation of two types of glazing on the one side of the bus.

Raymond Bell

The first Bristol REs for Citybus arrived in 1976 and introduced the new single-deck livery which was mainly ivory. Later in life several, including No 2060 seen here waiting on the Falls Road stop in Castle Street, had their galvanised steel bumper removed, giving the bus an unusual appearance. Compare No 2060 with No 2090, from the second batch delivered, in the photograph below, taken at the same location. *both Paul Savage*

Citybus vehicles undergo routine maintenance and servicing at their home depot but every few years they are taken to Falls Park workshops where they undergo a major overhaul. This usually includes a full repaint and here an almost complete No 2112 awaits the finishing touches. At this time No 2112 was a Falls-based bus, as indicated by the small 'F' above the fleet number. *Author*

One of the steepest climbs faced by buses in Belfast is that up Ballysillan Park, in the north of the city, to the Silverstream terminus. Here RE No 2120, with Ardoyne depot's Driver Elliman in command, struggles the last few yards to the turning area. The destination blinds have already been set for the return trip to Balmoral, off the Lisburn Road on the south side. Behind the bus are the hills above Knocknagoney and Stormont, to the east of the city.

Paul Savage

Looking tidy, on a private hire to Newtownards, is No 2315, one of the first batch of REs fiited with soft seating. Initially fitted with four-speed gearboxes they later received five-speed examples from Crosville and United REs. Number 2306 has been purchased by Messrs Shannon of Newtownards for preservation.

Paul Savage

The first Bristol RE to carry roof-mounted advertising boards, although on the nearside only at first, was No 2404. It is seen here crossing University Street into Botanic Avenue while on its way to the city centre and Carr's Glen.
Raymond Bell

Above: Royal Avenue again and 1980-built RE No 2409 heads across Castle Junction en route from Downview to the City Hall. It carries Buspak advertising panels. Similar No 2415 is preserved by the Irish Transport Trust (see page 151).
Paul Savage

Opposite: Donegall Square East is the location for this shot of Nos 2314 and 2059. Number 2059 was rebuilt at Falls Park as an engineering apprentice project after it had been hijacked in June 1984.
Paul Savage

Opposite: We move out to the east of the city now, to the Cherryvalley area. Number 2513 is turning from Cherryvalley Gardens on to the Gilnahirk Road on its way to the Gilnahirk terminus at Farmhurst Green. In the left background you should be able to see a Corporation bus stop. Cherryvalley Gardens is no longer served by Citybus, the route having been revised to run via Knock Road, King's Road and Gilnahirk Road. *Paul Savage*

Above: This is Castle Junction with RE No 2468 heading for Braniel via the Castlereagh Road. On 7 February 2005 the 32 service became Metro 5A. The building behind the bus once housed Robb's department store but was demolished and rebuilt as Donegall Arcade. *Paul Savage*

Opposite: The photographer's view has now changed completely and in 2005 you can no longer drive along this part of Chichester Street. Repeated attacks on the Royal Courts of Justice, to the left of the picture, led to the closure of the road and the construction of a security wall. Number 2522 is about to turn into Oxford Street on its way to Annadale via the Ravenhill Road. The last day of RE operation in Belfast, Saturday 31 January 2004, saw No 2522 working from Falls Park on routes to the west of the city. It was, however, failed, with defective demisters, after working the 1409 service 540 in from Twinbrook. *Paul Savage*

Opposite: On page 45 we featured one of the Plaxton Supreme IV-bodied Leyland Leopards transferred from Ulsterbus for use on private hire and city tours duties. Also used on city tours duties were a number of Bristol REs, including No 2563 seen here at the Manor House, Cultra whilst on a tour of the Belfast hills. These REs were fitted with public address systems for use on those duties. In 2005 Citybus no longer operate public city tours, these being provided by a private operator under the City Sightseeing banner. *Paul Savage*

Above: One of the last Bristol REs to enter service anywhere in the world was Citybus No 2559. Although not the last RE built it had been stored for several years before finally entering service in 1985. It was later fitted with an impact resistant flat glass windscreen and, at February 2005, was still owned by the company. It is seen here in Donegall Square West when new, ready to leave for Holywood Road and Knocknagoney. Look how deserted the streets are and it's only just after 6.30pm! Fortunately things have changed for the better (apart from the fact that the RE has gone). *Paul Savage*

Opposite: With so many vehicles Citybus was well placed to cope with large private hire events such as Orange Order demonstrations. Here No 2571 is at Laganbank Road, setting down participants from a Royal Black Preceptory demonstration on the last Saturday in August 1988. Several of the BXI-registered batch are now seeing further service in Co Donegal, with the Lough Swilly company (see photograph page 128). *Paul Savage*

Victims

Above: MH Coachworks-bodied Daimler Fleetline No 2703, which had been displayed at the Commercial Motor Show at Earl's Court in 1964, was destroyed in an attack on Ardoyne depot in 1980. Sister vehicle No 2586 sits alongside.
Raymond Bell

Opposite top: This is the top yard at Ardoyne depot, a place where many vehicles met their end. The only clearly identifiable vehicle is Alexander-bodied Atlantean No 2876, while four other Atlanteans and two Daimler Fleetlines can be distinguished. All credit must be given to Citybus staff as, even after events as serious as this, services were usually restored to their full level within a matter of days, often even hours.
Raymond Bell

Opposite bottom: It's Saturday 27 August 1988 and the remains of Bristol RESL No 729(2) lie at the side of the Falls Road awaiting the scrapman's attention. This bus was one of many hijacked and burned that day, there being about six others within several hundred yards of No 729(2). Number 729(2) can also be seen on page 107.
Mark O'Neill

Opposite: In the west of the city many vehicles were hijacked and destroyed on the Andersonstown Road. At that location we see Bristol RE No 2099, or rather the remains of it, being removed by a contractor, probably O'Neill.

Raymond Bell

Above: Ardoyne depot again and the remains of Bristol RE No 716(2), one of the two former United Counties examples, lies a twisted mass of melted metal waiting for the scrap man to come and tow it away. Also lost in this attack on 17 May 1988 was RE No 734(1) and No 2476 was damaged.

Mark O'Neill

Opposite: Bristol RE No 715(2), one of those acquired from Eastern National of Chelmsford, Essex was hijacked and set on fire at the junction of Springhill Avenue and Springfield Road on 11 March 1988. It is seen lying at that point awaiting the scrap man's attention.

Mark O'Neill

Rebuilt

Opposite: In addition to the vehicles taken over from the Corporation Citybus also took possession of 12 Daimler Fleetline chassis – 11 double-deck and one single-deck. The original MH Coachworks or Potter bodies on these chassis had been maliciously destroyed and new Alexander bodies, resembling the MH Coachworks design were constructed on nine of the double-deck chassis, these being 30'0" long examples. Number 2669 is seen here in Great Victoria Street, outside Shaftesbury Square Hospital, heading for Ladybrook on a journey diverted via the Lisburn Road due to disturbances on the Falls Road.
Raymond Bell

Above: Another rebuilt Fleetline was No 2595 which is seen at the Mount Merrion terminus at Rosetta Road, in the south of the city. The Alexander bodies, although similar to the original MH Coachworks design were constructed on aluminium frames, rather than steel and had rubber mounted glazing.
Raymond Bell

Opposite: As well as Fleetlines a number of Bristol REs were rebuilt, including No 2163, shown here at Malfin Drive, Taughmonagh, in the south of the city. Also of interest in this picture are the prefab bungalows. These have now disappeared as the whole area has been redeveloped. Just visible through the entrance door on No 2163 is the mounting for the ticket cancellers.
Author

The second-hand era
1 – The Fleetline interlude

Perhaps the most attractive of the many second-hand purchases were the 15 Fleetline single-deckers acquired in 1977 from Potteries Motor Traction of Stoke on Trent, hence their nickname amongst Citybus people – 'Stokes'. The attractive lines of these vehicles, with their panoramic windows, are well illustrated in this view of No 2935 in Chichester Street.
Raymond Bell

The 'Stokes' had Alexander bodies to the 'W' style, with large panoramic windows. They also featured soft seating and were regularly used on private hire duties. Number 2930 is seen at the Spelga Dam, high in the Mourne Mountains.

Raymond Bell

Possibly the worst vehicles purchased second-hand by Citybus were the 15 Daimler Fleetlines acquired from Northern General Transport of Gateshead, Tyne and Wear. Although bodied by a different builder (Willowbrook), these vehicles suffered from the same structural problems as the native Alexander-bodied examples.
Raymond Bell

This is Donegall Place, in the city centre, and Daimler Fleetline No 2948, ex Northern General, leads a line of vehicles waiting at the traffic lights. Number 2948 is working on the cross-town route from Ligoniel to Donegall Road, although this journey seems to be being curtailed at Celtic Park, perhaps due to disturbances on the Falls Road. Note, to the left of the picture, the security gates through which any vehicle entering the central area had to pass. *Raymond Bell*

The second-hand era
2 – The London connection (again!)

Above: Short Strand depot in the spring of 1977 and six of the AEC Merlins acquired from London Transport are lined up, ready for service. Apart from the addition of Citybus fleet numbers and the masking to the destination box to accommodate an RE style destination blind, little has been done to alter their London appearance. You might just be able to distinguish a lighter coloured panel, under the second window bay, where the London Transport name has been removed/painted over. *Raymond Bell*

Opposite: Two views – nearside and offside – of former London Transport 'MB class' AEC Merlins. Above, No 2518 rests in Upper Queen Street during a disruption to Falls Road services while No 2511 awaits its driver before heading for Oldpark. Both vehicles were new to London Transport in 1968 and had come to Citybus in 1980 from Ulsterbus. Both were withdrawn in 1981. The Citybus livery of red and trader ivory sat extremely well on these buses. Number 2511 was renumbered 673 in October 1981 and No 2518 became No 674 the same month.

both Paul Savage

Opposite: Parked up in Donegall Square East, just by the memorial to the Officers and men of the Royal Irish Rifles who died in the South African War (1899–1902), is AEC Merlin No 637, one of those acquired from London Country Bus Services of Reigate between April and August 1979. Formerly LCBS MBS 104, No 637 was one of the small number of Merlins operated which were built with a lower driving position. Compare this photograph with that of No 640 directly below. Number 637 was new in 1968, entered Citybus service in 1980 and was withdrawn in 1982.

Raymond Bell

Above: AEC Merlin No 2528 is from the second batch of vehicles purchased from London Transport in March 1977. It was of the 'MBS' standee type and was placed in service during June 1977. In order to release the fleet number for use on a new vehicle, it was renumbered to 675 in September 1981 and was finally withdrawn the following month. This photograph was taken at Carr's Glen and No 2528 is operating on the former trolleybus route to Cregagh.

Paul Savage

Opposite: When Falls Road services were disrupted due to marches, civil disturbance or security alerts Upper Queen Street could get a bit crowded. Here Merlin No 640, one of the London Country examples, leads a line-up of no fewer than seven former London vehicles.

Raymond Bell

Opposite: May 1977 saw the arrival of a batch of 15 'MB' type Merlins. Given fleet numbers 2506–20, all were allocated to the Ulsterbus fleet. Numbers 2511–3/7/8 were subsequently transferred to Citybus in March 1980. Number 2517 retained its Ulsterbus blue livery, with the addition of Citybus fleetnames and was used on the Royal Victoria Hospital Out-patients service, which at that time departed from Upper Queen Street. *Raymond Bell*

Above: An early example of the AEC Merlin, although one of the last batch to come to Belfast, was the former MBS 102, Citybus No 645, seen here picking up passengers outside the Belfast College of Technology en route to Glen Road, in the west of the city. Number 645 was new to London Transport in 1968 and came to Northern Ireland in 1979, entering public service the same year. It was withdrawn in 1981. *Raymond Bell*

Opposite: This caption might be a bit clearer if you look first at page 114! This is Upper Queen Street and AEC Merlin No 651 is pulling on to the stop to work a Turf Lodge service. Now resplendent in a coat of red and ivory No 651 had first operated in Belfast in full London Country colours, looking much as it had done on its last day in LCBS service. *Raymond Bell*

Opposite top: In May 1979 Citybus acquired four former London Transport 'MB class' Merlins which had been operated by Mid-Warwickshire Motors of Balsall Common. They were 1969-built vehicles and Citybus allocated them fleet numbers 2551–4. This is No 2551 which entered Citybus service in 1979. Alongside is native AEC Swift No 2766, in use on training duties. *Raymond Bell*

Opposite bottom: When London Transport couldn't supply any more Merlins Citybus took the shorter AEC Swift. Eighty were purchased but in the end only 69 actually saw public service. When the Swifts arrived in the Province they were normally taken to the Alexander factory at Mallusk where secure storage was available. They were then taken to Falls Park for overhaul before being returned to Mallusk to await a call to duty. Here freshly overhauled No 20 (SMS 546) rests at Mallusk, having just been returned from Falls. It retains London Transport livery but with aluminium-painted wheels. *Author*

Above: Alexander's again and Swift No 32, the former SMS 609, awaits a trip to Falls Park. It is just as it was on the last day that it ran in London. Some vehicles, like the one on the right of the picture, even arrived with full London destination blinds. To the front of No 32 is one of the ex-Northern General Daimler Fleetline single-deckers, repainted in Citybus red and ivory. *Author*

Opposite: Swift No 2, one of London Transport's 'SMS class', came to Northern Ireland from London in 1978 when it was around eight years old. It didn't last long being withdrawn in 1980. The Swift was a shorter version of the Merlin; compare this picture with that of Merlin No 651 on page 93. *Raymond Bell*

Above: This is No 79, the former London Transport SMD 446, seen in storage at the Alexander factory at Mallusk. Some stripping for parts seems to have already taken place. *Paul Savage*

Opposite: Following two disastrous firebomb attacks on Falls Park and Ardoyne depots in February 1980, claiming a total of 40 buses, 15 replacement vehicles were transferred to Citybus from the Ulsterbus fleet. Marshall-bodied former London Transport AEC Swift No 4 (EGN 206J) and Metro Cammell-bodied sisters Nos 13/7 (EGN 560/79J), 18 (EGN 608J) and 25 (EGN 594J) had originally been acquired by Citybus in 1978. They had subsequently been transferred to Ulsterbus to cover for heavy losses in the Londonderry City Services fleet. All were withdrawn in 1980, No 25 (EGN 594J) having been maliciously destroyed. This is No 17, seen at Ballyduff in company with an unidentified Leyland Atlantean. Note both Ulsterbus and Citybus style fleet number transfers have been applied. *Raymond Bell*

The second-hand era
3 – The Eastern Coach Works period

Above: The first Eastern Coach Works-bodied Bristol REs were acquired in 1980 and came from Crosville Motor Services of Chester. This is No 705, one of three which appeared in service with the area around the destination display painted ivory. They didn't stay like this for very long, being repainted into the red scheme as carried by No 706 opposite. The location for this picture is the turning circle at Ormeau. Initially standard Bristol RE destination blinds were cut to fit the narrower apertures on these vehicles and this led to some odd displays such as the 'ITY CENTR' seen here.
Author

Opposite top: Number 706 is seen here on the Upper Newtownards Road, just opposite the entrance to Knock Golf Club and is heading for the city centre, despite what is says on the front. The 16 route from Dundonald to the city centre via the Queen's Bridge disappeared with the introduction of the Metro network in February 2005.   *Ian Houston*

Opposite bottom: Freshly overhauled No 714, the former Crosville SRG 20, is seen at Falls Park workshops awaiting finishing touches. This was the first of three ECW-bodied REs to carry the number 714, the others coming from Eastern National of Chelmsford (see pages 44 and 104) and Wilts & Dorset, Poole (see title page).   *Paul Savage*

Opposite: Springmartin, in west Belfast, is the location for this picture of No 727, one of the vehicles acquired from United Automobile Services of Darlington in 1981. It was withdrawn in 1983. For many years the service from Springmartin was linked cross-town to the affluent suburb of Malone in the south of the city but that link was cut on 7 February 2005 with the introduction of the Belfast Metro network.
Paul Savage

Above: Number 738 was acquired from West Yorkshire Road Car in July 1981 and gave six years service to the city of Belfast. Advertising brings much needed income to bus operators and Citybus promoted the availability of advertising space using pictures of fruit and veg.
Paul Savage

Opposite: Two further RELL models arrived from United in January/February 1981. This one, the former United 4198, became Citybus No 731(1). It had been new in 1969. Seen here in a crowded Falls Park workshop it entered service later in 1981 and was withdrawn in 1983. The 'Shop at Binns' advert was once a familiar sight on buses in the northeast of England.
Paul Savage

Two Bristol RELLs came from East Midland Motor Services of Chesterfield in October 1984. Dating from 1972 they had been built with dual-door bodies but were later converted to single-door configuration. Number 775 is seen here in the yard at Falls Park depot. *Author*

Opposite: Another source of vehicles in the Yorkshire area was West Riding of Wakefield. Seven RELL models, including No 745, were purchased from this company in May 1983. Six of the seven buses dated from 1971, the seventh being a 1972 model. All were put into service during 1983, the last being withdrawn in 1988. The vehicle waiting behind is No 725, one of those acquired from United Auto. *Paul Savage*

The second ex-East Midland vehicle was given fleet number 776 by Citybus. It is seen here in the bus park at Falls Park depot, squeezed in amongst several native Alexander-bodied REs. Like so many other second-hand vehicles No 776 had a short life. Citybus placed it in service in 1985 and it was destroyed later the same year. Number 775 (opposite) was more fortunate, surviving until 1990. *Paul Savage*

Opposite: A new source of vehicles in 1985 was the Eastern National Omnibus Company of Chelmsford, Essex, which supplied five Bristol RELL models dating from 1970–2. All were eventually placed in service but this wasn't until 1987. Here No 792 waits outside the drivers' canteen in Donegall Square East. The building with the pillars is Donegall Square Methodist Church which in 2005 has changed uses to become the head office of the Ulster Bank. The sandstone building at the end of the block is the Pearl Assurance building. *Paul Savage*

Above: United Automobile Services, Darlington, was again the supplier of vehicles in November 1985 when five of its fleet, including OHN 462L, which became Citybus No 702(2), came to the Province. It is seen here in Wellington Place in company with native Bristol No 2560 which was an allover advert for the Coal Advisory Service. Number 702 first saw use in 1987 and was withdrawn in 1989. *Paul Savage*

Opposite: The number 714 was not a lucky one for Belfast's Eastern Coach Works Bristol REs, there ultimately being three which carried that number. Number 714(2) was probably the least fortunate of the three, never actually seeing passenger service, as it was hijacked on its way from Falls Park to Ardoyne where it was to replace a vehicle destroyed earlier (see picture on page 44). It is seen here, in happier times, arriving at Short Strand depot at the end of its journey from Eastern National at Chelmsford, Essex. *Author*

United Counties of Northampton supplied two REs with this style of Eastern Coach Works body featuring an unusual 'T-shaped' destination display in June 1987. Number 716(2) now appears for the second time in this book, albeit intact on this occasion (see page 83). The location for this picture is the now closed (and much missed) Ardoyne depot. *Mark O'Neill*

The second vehicle from United Counties was given fleet number 724(2). Seen here in the yard at Falls Park, it later returned to the Biggleswade area for preservation Sister vehicle No 716(2) unfortunately met a fiery end at Ardoyne depot (see photograph on page 83). *Paul Savage*

Bristol RESL No 729(2) was perhaps the oddest looking of the second-hand REs to be acquired, being the only RESL model with shallow, flat windscreens. It came from Crosville Motor Services of Chester in July 1987 and is seen at Falls Park depot still in National Bus Company green. It was new in 1968. *Author*

Before entering service No 729(2) was treated to a coat of red and trader ivory. It is seen here in Belfast's Castle Street shortly after entering service in 1988. It had a short life, being hijacked and burned out at the junction of Falls Road and Donegall Road later the same year. *Paul Savage*

Opposite: Fleet number 733 had remained unallocated due to there being a Daimler Fleetline numbered 2733; former Corporation drivers still referred to vehicles without the Citybus '2'! Once the Fleetline was withdrawn the number 733 became available and was allocated to a 1971 RESL model which arrived from Ribble Motor Services, Preston, in August 1987. It entered service in 1988 and was withdrawn in 1989. It is seen here at Falls Park following initial preparation for service, still wearing National Bus Company red but with the addition of red on white **CITYBUS** vinyls.

Paul Savage

Above: Fleet number 731(2) was a Leyland-engined engined Bristol RELL model which came to the Province in August 1987 having served with Cumberland Motor Services of Whitehaven, although it had been new to Bristol Omnibus. Whilst with Cumberland No 731(2), and its sisters, had worked on contracts based at the Sellafield nuclear plant. When this was discovered rumours began circulating that this batch of vehicles were lead lined or glowed in the dark.

Paul Savage

Opposite: Crosville Wales supplied four 1970 Bristol RELL6Gs in September 1987. Given fleet Nos 747–50(2), all were prepared for service in 1987/8, although they weren't used until 1988/9. Number 749(2), still wearing the Crosville Wales version of *Bws Gwynedd* livery is seen here at Falls Park being thoroughly overhauled. Numbers 747(2) (EFM 178H) and 748(2) (EFM 181H) returned to the mainland on withdrawal, No 747(2) for further use and No 748(2) for preservation (see page 153).

Paul Savage

United Automobile Services of Darlington supplied eight Bristol RESLs in March 1988 but only three, Nos 751–3(2) ever saw use in Northern Ireland. One of the three was No 751(2) but it only managed three weeks service before being withdrawn following a major mechanical failure.
Author

One of the later second-hand RE purchases was Leyland-engined No 773(2), which came from Yelloway Motor Services of Rochdale but had been new to a Welsh municipal operator, Aberdare, in 1972. It was prepared for service in 1988 and first saw use in August of the following year. It had a short life, being withdrawn by the end of 1989.
Paul Savage

The second Bristol RE to carry the number 778 was one of three acquired from Cambus in 1988, the previous holder of this number being a former United Auto vehicle (and featured on page 43). Number 778(2) is seen at Short Strand depot shorly after arriving from England. It was later painted into Citybus colours and allocated to the Driving School (see page 112) *Author*

Opposite: Occasionally the pressures caused by vehicle losses meant that the replacement vehicles had to be operated in their original owner's colours for a while. Citybus No 766(2) was a Bristol RESL which had been new to Ribble Motor Services of Preston and which came to Northern Ireland in April 1988. It ran for a time in the post-deregulation version of Ribble livery, complete with National Bus Company 'double N' symbol. It is seen here in Wellington Place in a view which shows just how few people ventured into the city centre for an evening's entertainment back in 1988. Note, too, the evidence of fire damage to the cant panels at the rear.
Paul Savage

Being fitted with high-backed coach-style seating No 778(2) was deemed unsuitable for service use and was consequently allocated to the Training School. On withdrawal it returned to England and is now preserved by a Mr Potts in Birmingham (see also page 152).
Paul Savage

This is No 779(2), one of three vehicles acquired from Cambus, Cambridge in September 1988. Being fitted with coach-style seating it was allocated to the training fleet. It later returned to England where it operated for Northern Bus as its No 2103 (see page 130). It is seen here at Short Strand shortly after delivery, still in Cambus pale blue livery.
Author

Possibly the worst of the second-hand REs to be acquired were two which came in November 1988 from West Sussex County Council, which had been using them as school buses. Originally five were expected but in the event only two turned up. New in 1972 to Trent Motor Traction of Stoke on Trent, both were in poor condition. Although allocated fleet Nos 780/2(2), neither was prepared for service and both were eventually sold for scrap in 1990. Number 780(2) was caught at Short Strand depot shortly after arriving in Northern Ireland. *Author*

Also acquired in November 1988 was a solitary vehicle from Kettlewell of Retford. New in 1972 to Bristol Omnibus, this vehicle was a Bristol RELH6L with Eastern Coach Works body fitted with 49 coach-style seats. The RELH chassis was a high frame version of the RE and was used primarily for vehicles used on long distance rural and motorway type work. This vehicle became fleet No 785(2) and although prepared for service, it was not used. As with the other coach-seated examples, it became a driver trainer in April 1989. It was withdrawn in 1990 and returned to the mainland for further use. *Author*

Emergencies

Former London Transport AEC Merlin MB 647, Citybus No 2544, was used on the *Citylink* service for a period in 1977. Apart from the addition of Citybus fleet numbers, legal lettering, a torn *Citylink* logo and the painting out of the LT names it is little changed from its London days. Even its LT fleet number may be glimpsed just to the right of the entrance door. The location for this picture is East Bridge Street and No 2544 is waiting in the bay just outside Central Station.
Raymond Bell

Former London Country AEC Merlin MBS 292 became Citybus No 651, although in this picture one couldn't exactly be sure of its ownership. Following a depot fire No 651 was taken from straight from the ferry and placed in service still in LCBS green. It was captured by the author collecting a good load of passengers at York Road Railway Station. *Author*

AEC Merlin No 2511, transferred from Ulsterbus in the spring of 1980, runs along Oxford Street en route to Central Station. The building to the left of the picture is the Royal Courts of Justice, now hidden behind a concrete wall. Number 2511 later received a coat of Citybus red and ivory paint. *Raymond Bell*

One of the oldest vehicles ever transferred/loaned to Citybus by Ulsterbus was Ulster Transport Authority-bodied Leyland Tiger Cub No 421, which was new in 1962. This photograph was taken at Lisburn depot and although No 421 is wearing a *Citylink* vinyl it is not thought to have actually been used by Citybus. *Author*

After serious losses in 1979 a number of vehicles destined for Ulsterbus were taken from Alexander's and used on the *Citylink* service, releasing standard vehicles for service elsewhere. One of the vehicles used was Bristol RE No 2377. It is seen in Donegall Square North, outside the now closed Robinson & Cleaver department store.
Raymond Bell

Leopard No 1146 was one of those acquired by Ulsterbus from Ribble Motor Services of Preston in July 1979. It carries bodywork by Marshall and was new in 1966. Apart from the addition of a *Citylink* vinyl on the front panel it still wears full Ulsterbus livery, complete with fleetnames.
Author

Ulsterbus Leyland Leopard No 169, which was to be allocated to Newtownards, also spent some time on the *Citylink* service. It is seen here at Central Station with the gasholder at Belfast Gas Works clearly visible in the background. The Gas Works site has been substantially cleared and has undergone a major redevelopment which includes a Radisson hotel and a Halifax call centre.
Author

As already mentioned on page 97, 15 vehicles were transferred from Ulsterbus in February 1980 to assist in the aftermath of two depot fires. Two unusual vehicles were Nos 1218/59, 45-seat Bedford VAM14s with Duple Northern bodies. Both tended to be used for private hire work or as engineer's runabouts. Number 1218 met a premature end in July 1980 when it was destroyed in a firebomb attack on Ardoyne depot. Number 1259 is seen at the City Hall in use by Short Strand depot's engineers.
Raymond Bell

RE replacements (or not!)

Above: Leyland B21 No 3002 was allocated to Ardoyne depot, where it was a popular bus with the drivers – probably because it was much faster than any Bristol RE! It could be found working on almost any route operated from that depot and is seen here turning from Chichester Street into Victoria Street in the city centre. In the distance the towers of the Scottish Provident building (left) and the Robinson and Cleaver building can be glimpsed. Number 3002 was sold to Ipswich Buses in 1991 and is now preserved. A photograph of it in Ipswich days can be seen on page 127.

Paul Savage

Opposite: The furthest point north reached by the tram, and later trolleybus, services of Belfast Corporation was the village of Glengormley. Following major housing developments in the area the bus services of the Corporation, and later Citybus, were extended beyond the village centre to the Ballyhenry and Carnmoney areas. In this July 1988 shot Lynx No 3006 is on an unusual 'short working' from the city centre to Glengormley only and having run 'round the block' it was about to return to the City Hall, despite what it says on the front. At Glengormley trolleybuses turned on a reverser which was located in the street just to the rear of No 3006.

Paul Savage

Number 3003 worked from Short Strand depot and was caught by our photographer at Ormeau terminus having worked through from Carr's Glen. It can just be glimpsed in the photograph of Bristol RE No 2464 at Carr's Glen on page 20.

Paul Savage

The first of the production Leyland Lynxes for Ulsterbus/Citybus was No 3007, which came to the Citybus fleet. It is seen here in Donegall Square West when brand new in June 1986. Beyond is Bristol RE No 2348 which wore a yellow-based scheme for the free shuttle service to the Co-op store on York Street.
Paul Savage

Of the five Lynxes initially allocated to Citybus No 3010 differed from the others in that it was Leyland, rather than Gardner, powered. It is seen here in Castle Place, once the departure point for trolleybus services to the Antrim Road. (See also photograph on page 127.)
Paul Savage

Opposite top: Four Lynxes, Nos 3007–10, were transferred on to the *Rail-Link* service in 1987 to replace Bristol REs Nos 2357–60. They were given a special livery based on that being applied at the time to certain of Northern Ireland Railways diesel electric multiple units. A smart No 3007 uplifts passengers at Central Station prior to its next journey to the city centre and York Road Station. Note the white on red destination blinds fitted to these vehicles. At the time of writing (March 2005), No 3007 is still in service with McGread of Omagh, Co Tyrone   *Paul Savage*

Opposite bottom: Taken from East Bridge Street, just outside Central Station, Lynx No 3008 is standing at the rudimentary facilities provided for passengers waiting on *Rail-Link* connections. Visible in the background, alongside platform 1, are a number of Northern Ireland Railways blue and grey-liveried BREL Mark 2 coaches which, presumably, were forming an 'Enterprise' working to Dublin's Connolly station.   *Paul Savage*

Rail links

Above: The first duty for Bristol RE No 2046 was on the *Citylink* service which connected Belfast's inappropriately-named Central Station to the city centre. The REs allocated to this service carried a special surround to the radiator grille, clearly visible in this shot of No 2046 on East Bridge Street, outside Central Station. The building in the background, now demolished and replaced by modern office accommodation, including a call centre for Abbey, was one of the Corporation Electricity Department's power stations.
Raymond Bell

Opposite: Bristol REs were regularly allocated to the *Citylink* duties and No 2212 is seen at Central Station when new in 1978. By this time the terminus had been relocated from the front of the building to this stop in the car park, just by the now closed Maysfield Leisure Centre.
Mark O'Neill collection

Several of the Potter-bodied AEC Swifts also spent some time on *Citylink* duties. Here No 2756 rests at Central Station before working through the city centre to York Road.
Raymond Bell

Above: The service to Central Station has followed several routes over the years. It once terminated outside the station (see photograph of No 2046 on page 122) and later at the lower level near Maysfield Leisure Centre. This latter point was reached by way of Laganbank Road and Mays Meadows. The photograph of Lynx No 3008 on page 121 was taken from the top of the bridge under which Bristol RE No 2359, in *Rail-Link* blue and grey, is passing. Note the route number, or rather letters, being displayed – CL for *Citylink*, despite the service being re-branded. Officially the route number was 100.

Author

Opposite: York Road railway station was much altered over the years and has now disappeared completely with the opening of the cross-harbour rail link in 1994. Lynx No 3009, in the dedicated NIR Suburban *Rail-Link* livery, awaits its passengers from a Larne line train.

Paul Savage

After wearing the blue and grey scheme Bristol RE No 2360 was repainted red and cream to act as a relief vehicle for the dedicated Leyland Lynxes. It is seen here in Donegall Place en route to York Road station. *Paul Savage*

Beyond Belfast

Already featured on page 8, prior to delivery to the Corporation, Daimler Roadliner No 2754 is seen here on the Isle of Man in its new role as a mobile church. Previously 754 UZ, it was re-registered MAN 528R during its stay on the island. It later returned to Northern Ireland, being noted in the Co Armagh area. It is believed to have been scrapped. Note the destination display – very appropriate to its role.
JD Howie

Opposite: Leyland's Lynx model did not prove to be a success in Northern Ireland and all were sold. Several, including No 3010, ended up with Stevenson's of Uttoxeter where they gave good service. On withdrawal a number returned to Ireland seeing service with Anchor Tours of Bellurgan Point, Co Louth. A picture of No 3010 with Citybus appears on page 120.
Author's collection (photographer unknown)

The Leyland B21s were sold to Ipswich Buses in 1991 and led full lives, the last being withdrawn in 2004. Ipswich No 151, the former Citybus No 3002, is now preserved on the mainland. *Author's collection (photographer unknown)*

After service with Stevenson's, and later Arriva, Leyland Lynx No 3006 returned to Ireland and a new owner, Keenan's t/a Anchor Tours. It is seen here at Keenan's premises at Bellurgan Point, Co Louth, still wearing Arriva colours on the front and also its Northern Ireland registration number. It spent most of its time on Bus Éireann schools contracts.

Author

Just as the Bristol RE was seeing out its last days with Ulsterbus/Citybus a number, including the former Citybus No 2577, were acquired by the well-known Co Donegal operator, the Lough Swilly Bus Company, where it became fleet number No 451. It is seen at Ireland's most northerly point, Malin Head, on 18 September 2004.

Paul Savage

When their Citybus days were over several Bristol REs were sold to Bus Éireann (as its 'BG class') for use on schools duties. Those with dual doors were converted to single door layout before sale and the seating capacity was also increased. The vehicles illustrated here are Citybus No 2045/Bus Éireann BG 13 (above) and Citybus No 2052/Bus Éireann BG 14 (below). BG 13 is seen at Dundalk garage, while the remains of BG 14 have been pushed to the back of the yard at Longford garage, having reached the end of its days. *Author (above)/Paul Savage (below)*

On withdrawal a number of the Eastern Coach Works-bodied REs were sold to Northern Bus of Dinnington. One was the former Citybus No 779, seen here being passed by a former Fylde Borough Transport Bristol RESL, while en route to Sheffield.
Author's collection (photographer unknown)

Number 785, the only Bristol RELH acquired by Citybus, also went to Northern Bus where it was allocated fleet number 2432.
Author's collection (photographer unknown)

Pennine Blue of Dukinfield operated Bristol RESL No 773 as its No 41. This vehicle had come to Citybus from Yelloway of Rochdale but had been new to Aberdare.
Author's collection (photographer unknown)

Citybus people

Management and Staff

The Head Office of Belfast Corporation Transport Department had been located at Utility Street, off Belfast's Donegall Road. On the commencement of Citybus operations in 1973 administration covering staffing, wages, finance, purchasing, claims, etc was centralized at the existing Ulsterbus Head Office at Milewater Road, to which location some of the former Corporation staff were relocated.

Engineering operations under Citybus continued along similar lines to that which had operated under the Corporation. Falls Park depot retained its Central Workshop position, dealing with annual vehicle overhauls and major accident damage. Day-to-day maintenance provisions were retained at Ardoyne and Short Strand depots, with similar provisions continuing at the front of Falls Park. A Chief Engineer was appointed, his responsibilities paralleling those of the Ulsterbus Chief Engineer.

Whilst significant differences existed between the terms and conditions of staff inherited from the Belfast Corporation Transport Department and existing Ulsterbus staff, many of these differences were eliminated early in Citybus days. However, certain aspects of the bus drivers terms of employment were to remain somewhat different from that applicable to Ulsterbus drivers throughout virtually the whole the Company's operational existence.

However, it was in the area of operational management that the greatest changes took place from that of the Corporation. On 'Day One', an Operations Manager was appointed, with responsibility for co-ordinating all operational activity and development, including financial control, whilst, following Ulsterbus practice, Depot Managers were appointed at each of the three Citybus depots. Their responsibilities included staff management, service provision, etc. The Operations Manager post ceased to exist as a separate entity in 1978 when the position of Central Area Manager (Ulsterbus) was expanded to include Citybus.

The following lists the managers who held the various posts during the period covered by this volume:

Chief Engineer	Tom Campbell	1973–88+
Operations Manager	Max Hale	1973–78
Central Area Manager	Max Hale	1978–83
	Tom Andrews	1983–88+
Depot Managers		
Ardoyne	Jim Orr	1973–76
	Eddie Rothwell	1976–88+*
Falls	Jim Orr	1973–75
	Wesley Snodden	1975
	Billy Hamilton	1975–88+
Short Strand	Ernie Neely	1973–81
	Frank Clegg	1982–85
	Frank Allen	1985–87
	Roy Sloan	1987–88+

Notes: Ardoyne and Falls both under Jim Orr 1973–75
+ indicates that these managers' tenure of office continued beyond the period covered by this volume
* also held the post of Chief Inspector during this period

Right: Ardoyne drivers Michael O'Hare and Billy Elliman (on bus) are seen with a Bristol RE, believed to be No 2224, at Balmoral.
Paul Savage

Left: Bill Loney, with trademark pipe, rests on the bumper of RE No 2227 at Springmartin. Bill also served as a driving instructor and spent some time in the Ulsterbus Tours pool too. *Paul Savage*

Above: Who said busmen weren't well paid? Frank Flannery, a Short Strand driver, poses alongside 'his' Lamborghini Countach at Four Winds terminus. (The luxury car actually belonged to a local businessman!)
Paul Savage

Left: As noted earlier the final working by an MH Coachworks-bodied Daimler Fleetline was a tour in No 2600 arranged by the Irish Transport Trust. The driver on that historic occasion was Peter Fusco. Peter went on to drive Scottish and continental tours for Ulsterbus.
Paul Savage

Right: Inspector Sammy Jeffers retired from Citybus in 2004. He started in career in public transport in 1964 as a conductor on the trolleybuses, before moving to driving. In 1968, on the withdrawal of the trolleys, he transferred to the diesel buses. He became an inspector in the mid 1980s.
Sammy Jeffers collection

Advertising vehicles

The early 1970s saw the emergence of the allover advertising livery, where the entire vehicle was painted into a specially designed scheme. The first such vehicle in the Citybus fleet, and indeed in Northern Ireland, was Daimler Fleetline/MH Coachworks No 2639 (639 EZ) which emerged in September 1974 in an allover advertisement for Pepsi. The vehicle retained this livery until November 1976 when it was returned to fleet livery. Only two other double-deckers were to receive allover advertising liveries – Leyland Atlanteans No 2877 (JOI 2877) for BEL 1 Furniture in September 1979 and No 2883 (JOI 2883) for Phoenix Assurance in July 1981. With the decline of the double-decker in the Citybus fleet attention now turned to the Bristol RE for future allover advertising vehicles.

For many years the panels between the upper and lower deck windows on double-deckers had been utilised as advertising space. In April 1977 the first of a new type of advertising vehicle appeared when Leyland Atlantean No 2897 (JOI 2897) emerged carrying a wrap around advert for the Trustee Savings Bank. In this case the advertisement was not only on the side panels but was also carried around the front and rear of the vehicle. Whilst more effective than traditional advertising, the concept never really caught on and only seven vehicles were to carry the wrap around adverts. These are detailed in the table below:

Fleet No	Reg No	Advert	From	To
2857	EOI 4857	Trustee Savings Bank	4/78	4/89
2877	JOI 2877	Bank Buildings	5/78	6/79
2884	JOI 2884	Ulster Cancer Foundation	8/77	9/79
2897	JOI 2897	Trustee Savings Bank	4/77	7/80
2899	JOI 2899	Trustee Savings Bank	10/81	10/82
2901	JOI 2901	Northern Bank Ltd	10/76	4/78
2903	JOI 2903	Northern Bank Ltd	10/77	7/80

Of the above, No 2897/9/901/3 were maliciously destroyed whilst still carrying the adverts.

One of the problems with having a largely single-deck fleet, is the lack of suitable space for advertising, an important source of revenue for bus companies. In an effort to combat this, Citybus had Bristol RE No 2404 (VOI 8404) fitted with roof mounted advertising panels in 1982. These were known as 'Skybreakers' and the experiment was obviously a success, as in 1983 a further 39 vehicles, Nos 2330–9 (UOI 2330–9) and 2401–3/5–30 (VOI 8401–3/5–30), received the advertising panels, by now renamed 'Buspak' panels, after the company then contracted to supply advertising to Citybus vehicles. Number 2404 had the prototype panels removed at this time and replaced by standard panels.

In 1984 a further six vehicles were fitted with Buspaks. Two were fitted on allover advertising vehicles, Nos 2487 (XOI 2487) and 2531 (AXI 2531), at the request of the customer and the other four were on the vehicles used on the Northern Ireland Railways *Rail-link* service which linked the city's railway stations with the city centre, these being Bristol REs Nos 2357–60 (UOI 2357–60). Only two sets of these panels were in fact new, the others being removed from No 2336 (UOI 2336) and Nos 2408/12/4 (VOI 8408/12/4). A further 25 sets of panels were fitted in 1985 to Nos 2490–2500/2–12/5 (XOI 2490–2500/2–12/4) and 2534/41 (AXI 2534/41). Of these No 2515 (XOI 2515) and Nos 2534/41 (AXI 2534/41) were allover advertising vehicles, the panels on Nos 2534/41 (AXI 2534/41) having been removed from No 2337 (UOI 2337) and No 2430 (VOI 8430).

In an effort to spread the appropriate message, several advertising-liveried vehicles were loaned to Ulsterbus at various times. Bristol RE No 2531 (AXI 2531) operated on Londonderry City Services between April 1985 and June 1986 and RE No 2541 (AXI 2541) was similarly employed between July 1986 and September 1987. Another Bristol RE, No 2560 (AXI 2560), also operated on Londonderry City Services from August 1985 to September 1986 before moving to Craigavon where it remained until April 1987. It returned to Londonderry for a final loan period in February 1988 where it remained until it was hijacked and destroyed in August 1989.

Daimler Fleetline No 2857 was one of three vehicles to receive wrap around adverts for the Trustee Savings Bank, the others being Leyland Atlanteans Nos 2897 and 2899. This shot, taken in Donegall Square East, with the Scottish Provident building as a backdrop, has another vehicle of interest just to the rear of No 2857. It was one of a number of Austin FX4 taxicabs used by Citybus inspectors to monitor services around the city. *Paul Savage*

Leyland Atlantean No 2899 also carried a wrap around advert for the Trustee Savings Bank, although in a different style. It is seen in Wellington Place about to head for Ligoniel on route 55 via Shankill Road, a journey that it is no longer possible to make. Number 2899 replaced similar No 2897 which had been maliciously destroyed.
Paul Savage

Opposite: The first allover advertising liveried Citybus to appear on the streets of Belfast was MH Coachworks-bodied Daimler Fleetline No 2639 which carried a blue and white based scheme for Pepsi. It wore these colours for just over two years from 1974 to 1976. This view was taken at Short Strand depot.

Raymond Bell

Above: The Co-op store on York Street was a popular place for Belfast shoppers but it was away from the main shopping area. To encourage shoppers a free shuttle bus was provided using, first, Bristol RE No 2341 then No 2348 in a dedicated yellow livery. It is seen here leaving Donegall Place and crossing Castle Junction into Royal Avenue. Just to the left of the picture is a place familiar to many transport enthusiasts, the much missed Mullan's Bookshop.

Paul Savage

Opposite: Seen inside the workshop area at Ardoyne depot in the summer of 1981 is Leyland Atlantean No 2883, freshly repainted into an allover blue-based advertising scheme for Phoenix Assurance. The symbol of a phoenix rising from the ashes was perhaps somewhat appropriate for an Ardoyne-based bus given the number of firebomb attacks this depot suffered. This vehicle was a particular favourite of Bill Loney, who appears on page 132 and who regularly used it on training duties.

Paul Savage

The marketing people at the Coal Advisory Service must have liked the idea of allover advertising buses as they took five. This is RE No 2560, which was later destroyed in Londonderry. *Ian Houston*

One of the brightest schemes applied to an allover advertising bus was that on Bristol RE No 2554 which promoted the local ITV station, Ulster Television. Wearing its spacescape-based livery, with rainbow stripes, No 2554 is seen here catching the light in the Braniel estate. *Raymond Bell*

The following is a list of allover advertising vehicles and contracts during the period covered by this book:

Fleet No	Reg No	Advert	From	To
2639	639 EZ	Pepsi Cola	9/74	11/76
2877	JOI 2877	BEL 1 Furniture	9/79	6/84
2336	UOI 2336	Ross Poultry (Day-lay Eggs)	4/80	1/81
2348	UOI 2348	Co-op Shuttle	6/80	8/87
2883	JOI 2883	Phoenix Assurance	7/81	2/84
2549	AXI 2549	Isaac Agnew	4/83	6/84
2555	AXI 2555	New Dimension Furniture	7/83	2/86
2357/8	UOI 2357/8	NIR *Rail-link*	8/83	6/87
2359	UOI 2359	NIR *Rail-link*	8/83	11/87
2360	UOI 2360	NIR *Rail-link*	8/83	12/87
2560	AXI 2560	Coal Advisory Service	9/83	8/89
2558	AXI 2558	Nectar Cosmetics	10/83	3/85
2515	XOI 2515	RE Hamilton	1/84	10/84
2531	AXI 2531	Youth Training Programme	3/84	6/86
2483	XOI 2483	Fountain Shopping Centre, Belfast	7/84	9/86
2487	XOI 2487	Coal Advisory Service	8/84	3/88
2549	AXI 2549	Calor/Kosangas	2/85	3/88
2526	XOI 2526	Coal Advisory Service	4/85	3/90
2541	AXI 2541	Youth Training Programme	4/85	8/87
2534	AXI 2534	Coal Advisory Service	5/85	9/89
2536	AXI 2536	JT Minimix	6/85	6/88
2558	AXI 2558	JT Minimix	9/85	6/88
2515	XOI 2515	Energy Efficiency Year 1986	11/85	6/87
2555	AXI 2555	Youth Training Programme	4/86	6/87
2538	AXI 2538	Finlandia Vodka	6/86	8/87
2554	AXI 2554	Ulster Television	7/86	10/89
2483	XOI 2483	YMCA	11/86	4/88
2531	AXI 2531	Youth Training Programme (2)	5/87	10/88
3007–10	HXI 3007–10	NIR *Rail-link*	6/87	9/91
2360	UOI 2360	NIR *Rail-link* (2)	7/87	12/88
2515	XOI 2515	BBC Inside Ulster	8/87	12/92
2555	AXI 2555	BBC Radio Ulster	8/87	7/88
2541	AXI 2541	Coal Advisory Service	11/87	5/92
2383	UOI 2383	Coal Advisory Service	4/88	10/92
2483	XOI 2483	Northern Ireland Airports Duty Free	5/88	6/89
2536	AXI 2536	Creations Furniture	9/88	1/91
2558	AXI 2558	Century 21 Estate Agents	9/88	8/90
2531	AXI 2531	Creations Furniture	12/88	12/90

Notes:

Number 2383 (UOI 2383) was transferred from the Ulsterbus fleet in 3/88 and was repainted into an allover advertising livery for the Coal Advisory Service. It returned to Ulsterbus in 5/88 without ever seeing service with Citybus.

Numbers 2487 (XOI 2487), 2555 and 2560 (AXI 2555/60) were all maliciously destroyed whilst still carrying allover advertising liveries; No 2560 (AXI 2560) was on loan to Ulsterbus at the time.

Driver training vehicles

In the latter years of the Belfast Corporation Transport Department, and in the early days of Citybus, no specific vehicles were allocated to driver training duties, vehicles being drawn from the service fleet as and when required.

It was to be July 1979 before Citybus set up a dedicated driver training fleet when three of the MH Coachworks-bodied Daimler Fleetlines, Nos 2581/6/97 (581/6/97 EZ), were assigned to training duties. The most noticeable change in the appearance of these vehicles was the panelling over of the destination display and the fitting of appropriate signage to indicate to the public that they were employed on training duties. Number 2586 was destroyed in a firebomb attack on Ardoyne depot in February 1980 and was not replaced. Numbers 2581/97 remained in use until November of the same year when they were replaced by sister vehicles Nos 2585/7 (585/7 EZ). Number 2585 only lasted six months before being withdrawn and in April 1982 No 2587 was joined by former Citybus Potter-bodied Daimler Fleetline No 2712 (712 UZ), which had latterly been operating for Ulsterbus at Coleraine. Both remained in use until May 1983 and during its period as a training vehicle No 2712 retained Ulsterbus livery. Number 2712 almost survived into preservation, being owned for a short time by the Irish Transport Trust. However a seized engine finally sealed its fate and it was subsequently sold for scrap.

Replacements for Nos 2587 and 2712 came in the shape of two of the 33'0" long Alexander-bodied Daimler Fleetlines, Nos 2825/49 (AOI 825/49). Number 2849 was withdrawn in January 1988 following accident damage and was replaced by similar No 2863 (EOI 4863). Numbers 2825/63 were to be the last double-deckers to fulfil the dedicated driver training role, being replaced in 1989 by several of the second-hand Eastern Coach Works-bodied Bristol REs. For No 2825 it was the end of the road but No 2863 returned to passenger service in May 1991, converted to open-top for use on city tours, private hire and promotional work. It was to fulfil this role for nearly nine years before being finally withdrawn in 2003 and sold for scrap.

During the period under review, a number of the Potters-bodied AEC Swifts and former Potteries Motor Traction Alexander-bodied Daimler Fleetline single-deckers were allocated to the training fleet for short periods. No permanent modifications were carried out on these vehicles and all were capable of being used in normal service if required. In addition normal service vehicles continued to be drafted in, as and when needed, to augment the training fleet.

Opposite: Accidents can happen to training buses just as easily as they can to ordinary service buses as witnessed by No 2849 lying withdrawn at the back of Falls Park depot. Note the damage to the roof dome. For its role as a trainer No 2849 was fitted with an additional window immediately behind the cab. This was to increase the instructor's field of view.

Author

The first vehicles dedicated solely to training duties were three of the MH Coachworks-bodied Daimler Fleetlines – Nos 2581/5/97. This is No 2597 and was caught by the photographer turning from Howard Street into Great Victoria Street, with Church House in the background. Number 2597 is looking a bit the worse for wear in this shot.

Raymond Bell

Service vehicles

Towing vehicles

In 1948/9 Belfast Corporation's Transport Department had acquired five AEC Monarch tower wagons, Nos TW52–56 (MZ 2321–5), to maintain the tram and trolleybus overhead wiring. In addition to tending to the needs of the tram and trolleybus fleet, they also doubled as towing vehicles for the motorbus fleet. As first the tramway system and then the trolleybus system declined and finally closed, the need for these vehicles greatly reduced and by the time Citybus came into existence, only two, Nos TW53/6, remained in traffic and had been officially renumbered RV53/6 to reflect their status as recovery vehicles (although RV53 still carried TW53 to the end of its days).

One major problem associated with these vehicles was that they were only of use when recovering vehicles that could be brought in on a towing bar; no facility existed for recovering vehicles that required a suspended tow. To remedy this situation a Ford D series recovery vehicle, with Holmes lifting gear, was acquired in 1975. Numbered RV57 and registered JOI 1875, it replaced No RV56 (MZ 2325), which was sold on to Miller, Castlereagh, one of a number of dealers who were taking scrap Citybus vehicles at the time. Number RV56 was used for a while to tow vehicles on their final journey to Millers scrapyard in the Castlereagh Hills, overlooking Belfast, before being finally broken up itself.

For many years most Ulsterbus depots had operated their own recovery vehicle for tow-ins, with a specialised recovery crane based at Duncrue Street works for suspended tows. (Most of the towcars were conversions from former buses.) Three former Ulsterbus UTA-bodied Leyland Tiger Cubs, Nos 428/58/80 (7428/58/80 CZ), were transferred to Citybus in 1981 for conversion to towing vehicles. Of these No 480 was painted in an allover maroon scheme with yellow and black chevrons on the front and rear and was placed in service at Falls Park depot where it ousted the last of the AEC Monarchs, No RV53 (MZ 2322). The remaining two Tiger Cubs received Citybus red and ivory livery, again with chevrons front and rear, before being placed in service at Short Strand (428) and Ardoyne (458).

The availability of more modern vehicles saw the three Tiger Cubs moved on in 1984/5, their replacements, also coming from Ulsterbus, being Alexander-bodied Bedford YRQs Nos 1717/63/84 (HOI 1717/63/84). Number 1763, based at Short Strand depot, was the only one of the trio to receive Citybus livery, No 1717, based at Falls Park depot and No 1784, based at Ardoyne depot, retained Ulsterbus blue and ivory for the rest of their working lives. The Bedfords remained in use until 1993/4 when they in turn were replaced by newer vehicles.

Opposite: Leyland Tiger Cub No 480 is seen at Glenwood Street, on the Shankill Road, assisting with the recovery of a broken down Leyland Atlantean. It being passed by Daimler Fleetline No 2846, en route for Glencairn. Number 480 has obviously been in the wars; note the panelled over windows and the windscreens replaced with flat glass rather than the original curved style. Of the three Tiger Cubs used for towing only No 480 wore this maroon scheme; Nos 428 and 458 both received standard red and ivory.
Raymond Bell

Belfast Corporation Transport had five of these AEC Monarch tower wagons which were used in the maintenance of the tram and trolleybus overhead wiring. Despite being officially re-numbered RV 53, TW 53 still carried its original number in this 1980s view at Falls Park depot. Tram lines are just visible, directly in front of the vehicle. *Paul Savage*

Ford D series RV 57 was acquired in 1975 to provide a facility for vehicles requiring a suspended tow. It is seen here at Falls Park, having recovered Daimler Fleetline No 2573, albeit on a bar.

Ian Houston

The Leyland Tiger Cubs were replaced with three Alexander-bodied Bedford YRQs, also from the Ulsterbus fleet. Short Strand depot's No 1763 is pictured returning to its home base with a broken down Bristol RE in tow. Number 1763 was the only one of the three to gain Citybus red, the others operating in Ulsterbus blue throughout their lives.

Author

Perhaps the most unusual vehicle ever to carry a Citybus fleetname was this Thornycroft mobile crane, fleet number TC 75 (TZ 4184), which came from the Corporation. It was used occasionally on breakdown duties and I have a recollection of seeing it in Donegall Place lifting a Fleetline to allow a wheelskate to be fitted. It is seen here at Duncrue Street yard during a period when vehicles were evacuated from depots.

Raymond Bell

Fare Structure and Ticket Systems

The fare structure inherited by Citybus from Belfast Corporation was an unusual two-zone system that had been introduced in February 1970, with the intention of speeding up fare collection with one-man operation. Passengers were encouraged to pay their fares with tokens that could be purchased in advance from ticket agents at a discounted price. Passengers with tokens inserted these into a machine on the bus, which issued a ticket showing the boarding stage and time. The ticket was similar in appearance to those issued by the Bell Punch 'Ultimate' ticket dispensers introduced for one man operation at the same time. (Belfast Corporation had used 'Ultimate' ticket dispensers before, from 1950 to 1959, when they were replaced by TIM registers.) Passengers without tokens paid the driver in cash. Journeys were priced on a coarse scale of either one or two tokens, replacing a finer scale of five fare values, depending on the journey length. During the planning stage it had been intended to have three fares, one 'S' token, one 'M' token or two 'S' tokens. 'S' presumably stood for short and 'M' for medium distance. However this complication was dropped and the 'M' tokens were used for concession journeys. Another plan was that passengers paying cash fares would be sold tokens which they would then have to insert in the token machines. Fortunately this complication was also dropped before the launch, but was the reason why both 'S' and 'M' tokens were produced in two types – round and multi-sided.

By the time Citybus took over responsibility for the Belfast Corporation system, it was becoming apparent that the self service layout meant that many passengers were paying with only one token, but remaining on board to travel for a two token journey, a form of Fare Evasion known as over riding. Clearly the resultant loss of revenue was contributing to the financial woes of the Corporation Transport department, and was one of the problems which had to be tackled by the new management team. Only one other British transport undertaking, Sunderland Corporation, was using tokens for the payment of fares at this time. This system was fairly short lived as it was withdrawn following the absorption of that undertaking into the Tyne and Wear PTE. Some of their token machines were later acquired by Citybus to replace equipment destroyed with buses.

After careful consideration, Managing Director Werner Heubeck decided to move to a flat fare system, reasoning that if passengers paid one fare on entering the bus, that would be the only fare and over riding would be abolished. At the same time he intended to replace the token system with multi-journey tickets which passengers would cancel on entering the bus. He carried out extensive research among operators in continental Europe, where the flat fare system and multi-journey tickets were almost universal. This, together with his own extensive knowledge of paper making, in which industry he had worked before joining Ulsterbus in 1967, determined the policy that tickets should not be either folded or clipped during the cancelling process, both being systems in widespread use in Europe. He personally devised the square format ticket which, stamped on both faces and all sides, would permit eight journeys to be made. This determined the type of ticket cancellors specified for the conversion, which was introduced in April 1978, preceded by a publicity campaign featuring cartoons of Werner Heubeck himself, drawn by Belfast Telegraph cartoonist Rowel Friers.

Unfortunately fare evasion was not entirely abolished, as some passengers realised that the tickets could be reused repeatedly, or the ticket cancellors ignored altogether. Whilst this problem had been recognised by the mid 1980s and special surveys were conducted to evaluate the revenue loss, the introduction of measures to tackle the problem was one of the first actions implemented by Werner Heubeck's successor, after his retirement in November 1988.

1

2

9

3

4

5

7

6

8

Opposite: **1** and **2** – Tickets ('S' – pink, 'M' – yellow) issued from the token operated machines illustrated at figs 8 and 9. Tickets marked 'Belfast Corporation Transport Department' were still in use until 1978.
3 to 7 – Tickets issued by drivers from an 'Ultimate' ticket machine, seen in fig 8. 'S' and 'M' were driver issues in case of token machine failure, 'A' (blue) was for the adult cash fare, 'C' (green) for the child and 'O.A.P.' (grey) for senior citizen fares.
8 – 'M' token machine (yellow) and 'Ultimate' ticket machine as fitted to a 28xx-series Daimler Fleetline
9 – 'S' token machine (red) as fitted to Bristol RE No 2101. The stand for the new ticket canceller has already been fitted behind.

1 to 7 – Paul Savage
8 and 9 – Author

Monday 3 April 1978 saw the replacement of the token system, introduced by the Corporation in 1970, with a continental style system where passengers cancelled their own tickets. An advertising campaign featured a cartoon of Managing Director, Werner Heubeck. This advert was carried on bus sides, next to the entrance door, this one being on Bristol RE No 2101.
Author

The new multi-journey tickets were designed by Werner Heubeck himself; he had worked previously in the paper industry and his knowledge of that determined the style of ticket to be used. Tickets could be used on both sides allowing up to eight journeys to be made. The tickets immediately to the right were early issues – orange for adults and green for concession. Later issues featured a white border, or a lighter colour, to aid visibility. Close inspection of the ticket with the white border will reveal a security feature – Citybus mispelled CTIYBUS!

The stamp on the ticket gave details of the journey being made. Taking journey no 5 on the ticket with the white border as an example – 763 is the machine number, O173 indicates an outward journey, from the central zone, on route 73, which was made on 28 January at 1710.
Paul Savage

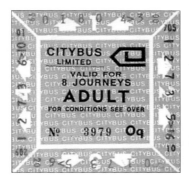

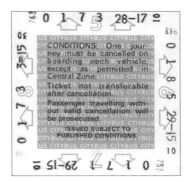

Left and above: These cartoons by Rowel Friars appeared in the publicity booklet for the introduction of multi-journey tickets.

Timetable covers from 1983 and 1988 showing a Bristol LH, a type never operated by Citybus and Bristol RE No 2361, one of those transferred in from Ulsterbus.

In preservation

You will probably be surprised to see how many vehicles that were operated by Citybus during the period 1973–88 are, or were, preserved. The list below includes vehicles inherited from Belfast Corporation Transport Department, along with those built new for Citybus or acquired second-hand. Not all vehicles are fully restored and some no longer exist, having been subsequently sold or scrapped. The dates in brackets indicate the year purchased for preservation.

Guy Arab III/Harkness	2346 (1975)
Daimler CVG6/Harkness	2432 (1975), 2446 (1976)
Daimler Fleetline/MH Coachworks	2596b (1980), 2600b (1981)
Daimler Fleetline/Potter	2712b (1984)
Daimler Fleetline/Alexander	2857 (1995)
AEC Swift/Park Royal	75 (1981)
AEC Merlin/MCW	678 (1982)
Bristol RE/Alexander	2151 (2003), 2156 (2003), 2288 – chassis only (1992), 2306 (2004), 2316 (2003), 2415 (1997), 2531 (2003), 2534 (2004), 2542 (2004), 2565 (2003)
Bristol RE/ECW	724(2) (1990), 728(2) (1990), 732(2)a (1994) then preserved again 2004, 741(2) (1992), 748(2) (1990), 764(2) (1992), 766(2)b (1995), 773(2)b (1994), 778(2) (1994)
Leyland B21/Alexander	3002 (2002)

Notes

A (2) after the fleet number indicates that this was the second vehicle of that type to carry that fleet number
a   subsequently sold out of preservation
b   subsequently scrapped

Raymond Bell's 1950 Guy Arab III/Harkness No 346, served with Citybus as its No 2346 and has featured already, on page 7. It was withdrawn in 1975 and underwent a major restoration. It is currently receiving another major ovehaul and should make a reappearance in 2005.
Paul Savage

Opposite: In 1952/3 Belfast Corporation purchased 98 Daimler CVG6s and 2 Daimler CVD6s, all bodied locally by Harkness. One of the last to remain in service was No 446, by then re-numbered 2446. On withdrawal in 1975 it passed into preservation and is now owned by Jonathan Miller of Belfast. It is seen here at the Balmoral Show Grounds (King's Hall) turning circle in the mid 1980s, when on an enthusiasts outing. Number 446 carries Corporation colours, complete with coat of arms.
Paul Savage

Above: Displaying an appropriate destination, the Irish Transport Trust's Bristol RE No 2415, crosses the bridge at Conwy, North Wales, with Conwy Castle behind, on its way to the Transport Festival at Llandudno in May 2000. Number 2415 was new in 1980 and is the sole surviving dual-door Citybus Bristol RE. Of the 205 built new for Citybus over 70% were maliciously destroyed.
Paul Savage

Opposite: Citybus No 724(2), the former United Counties No 319, returned, on withdrawal, to the mainland for preservation and was last recorded with a Mr Robertson of Biggleswade. It is seen here at Duxford, home of Britain's biggest bus rally, Showbus, in 2000. By this time it had been adorned with a coat of National Bus Company (NBC) leaf green paint and a set of NBC style fleetnames. A reminder of its Citybus days is the amount of plain glass fitted to the side windows. Sister vehicle No 716(2), United Counties No 330, appears is a less happy state on page 83.
Paul Savage

Citybus Bristol RE No 778(2), featured on pages 111 and 112, returned to England on withdrawal and is now preserved in the Birmingham area by a Mr Potts. It has been restored to the livery of its original operator, Eastern Counties, and was caught by our photographer working on a free service at the 2003 Llandudno Transport Festival. In the background is a former Bristol Omnibus Company Bristol KSW, along with a former Merseyside PTE Leyland Atlantean.

Paul Savage

Ribble Bristol RESL No 338 became Citybus No 764(2) (see page 49). It was sold in 1992 and has now been superbly restored to 'as delivered' condition. Now owned by the Ribble Vehicle Preservation Trust, it has been the recipient of many awards and commendations and is seen here at the 2004 Showbus event at Duxford where it won the 'Best Preserved Bus' category.

Paul Savage

A former Crosville Bristol RE, now owned by the SRG Group based in the Runcorn area, is the one time Citybus No 728(2). It has been restored to National Bus Company colours but wears the special version, with a broad orange band which incorporates a large 'T', that was applied to vehicles working services on the Runcorn busway. It was posed alongside a former stablemate, the Irish Transport Trust's No 2415, at an earlier Llandudno Transport Festival.
Paul Savage

Citybus acquired several batches of vehicles from Crosville Motor Services but this one came from Crosville Wales, based at Llandudno. Crosville Wales was one of the companies formed from the privatisation of the National Bus Company. Crosville SRG 181 became Citybus No 748(2) and is seen here back on home ground at the Llandudno Transport Festival. It is now owned by the same group which have No 728(2) and has been restored to National Bus Company livery.
Paul Savage

Fleet list

The fleet list is divided into several sections. The first table lists in numerical order the official operational fleet inherited from Belfast Corporation Transport Department on 2 April 1973. Buses built new for Citybus from 1973 to 1988 are in the fourth table, broadly in chronological order. The eighth table comprises pre-owned vehicles purchased by Citybus, in the majority of cases to replace vehicles lost due to civil disturbance. Since there are over many hundreds of vehicles are in these lists, the general descriptive data for each group of vehicles is presented in summary form, including a general indication of the longevity of each type in normal passenger service. Each section is followed by individual listing of those vehicles withdrawn from normal service during the period covered by this book. Vehicles continuing in service beyond 1988 will be listed in Volume 6 in this series. Withdrawal dates quoted refer to final withdrawal from normal passenger service. Many withdrawn vehicles remained in company ownership for lengthy periods, either held in reserve or as a source of spare parts. Code letters attached to the withdrawal year are explained at the start of the first such list. Appendices following the fleet list show vehicles retained for other active uses, ie towing, training and staff transport, with relevant dates. Another appendix lists the surplus vehicles inherited from BCT for disposal.

PSV Circle codes to describe bodywork and seating are used in the column headed 'Seats' and are explained as follows:

B	Bus seating	F	Front or forward entrance
C	Coach seating	D	Dual doorway (front entrance/centre exit)
DP	Dual-purpose (coach seating in bus body)	R	Rear entrance
H	High-bridge double decker	RD	Rear entrance with door
L	Low-bridge double decker	T	Toilet
OT	Open-top double decker		

(Seating of double deckers is quoted as upper deck followed by lower deck.)

Where the symbol 'xxx' appears in the Reg No column, this indicates that the numbers on the plates do not run in sequence. The word 'various' indicates that the registration letters also vary. In both instances full details for individual vehicles will be found in the withdrawal lists.

Suffixes used in the withdrawal lists:

a	withdrawn due to accident
f	withdrawn with accidental fire damage
m	withdrawn due to malicious damage/destruction
n.o.	not operated
p	preserved
r	retained as garage towing vehicle
s	sold to another operator
t	retained as driver training vehicle
ub	transferred to Ulsterbus

Citybus vehicles inherited from BCT on 2 April 1973

Fleet Nr	Reg Nr	Built	Chassis Type	Body Type	Seats	Wdn
2306/7	MZ 7404/5	1950	Guy Arab III	Harkness	H28/26R	1974/75
2309–11	MZ 7407–09	1950	Guy Arab III	Harkness	H28/26R	1975
2322/3	MZ 7420/1	1950	Guy Arab III	Harkness	H28/26R	1975
2326–30	MZ 7424–28	1950	Guy Arab III	Harkness	H28/26R	1974/75
2332–37	MZ 7430–35	1950	Guy Arab III	Harkness	H28/26R	1974/75
2341	MZ 7439	1951	Guy Arab III	Harkness	H28/26R	1974
2343/4	MZ 7441/2	1951	Guy Arab III	Harkness	H28/26R	1975
2346–48	MZ 7444–46	1951	Guy Arab III	Harkness	H28/26R	1975
2350–52	OZ 6604–06	1952	Daimler CVG6	Harkness	H30/26R	1973/74
2355	OZ 6609	1952	Daimler CVG6	Harkness	H30/26R	1974
2364	OZ 6618	1952	Daimler CVG6	Harkness	H30/26R	1973
2366/7	OZ 6620/1	1952	Daimler CVG6	Harkness	H30/26R	1973–75
2372	OZ 6626	1952	Daimler CVG6	Harkness	H30/26R	1975
2376/7	OZ 6630/1	1952	Daimler CVG6	Harkness	H30/26R	1973/74
2379–81	OZ 6633–35	1952	Daimler CVG6	Harkness	H30/26R	1973–75
2386	OZ 6640	1953	Daimler CVG6	Harkness	H30/26R	1973
2389–94	OZ 6643–48	1953	Daimler CVG6	Harkness	H30/26R	1973–75
2397	OZ 6651	1953	Daimler CVG6	Harkness	H30/26R	1974
2408/9	OZ 6662/3	1953	Daimler CVG6	Harkness	H30/26R	1973–75
2411–13	OZ 6665–67	1953	Daimler CVG6	Harkness	H30/26R	1973
2415	OZ 6669	1953	Daimler CVG6	Harkness	H30/26R	1973
2418–28	OZ 6672–82	1953	Daimler CVG6	Harkness	H30/26R	1973–75
2431/2	OZ 6685/6	1953	Daimler CVG6	Harkness	H30/26R	1973–75
2434–37	OZ 6688–91	1953	Daimler CVG6	Harkness	H30/26R	1975
2439/40	OZ 6693/4	1953	Daimler CVG6	Harkness	H30/26R	1973–75
2442–44	OZ 6696–98	1953	Daimler CVG6	Harkness	H30/26R	1973–75
2446	OZ 6700	1953	Daimler CVG6	Harkness	H30/26R	1975
2447–48	OZ 6701/2	1954	Daimler CVG6	Harkness	H30/26R	1974/75
2551	5540 XI	1960	Leyland Atlantean PDR1/1	Alexander	H43/34F	1975
2553–58	553–58 EZ	1962	Daimler Fleetline CRG6	MH Coachworks	H44/31F	1976/77
2562–80	562–80 EZ	1962	Daimler Fleetline CRG6	MH Coachworks	H44/31F	1973–80
2581	581 EZ	1963	Daimler Fleetline CRG6	MH Coachworks	H44/31F	1979
2583–94	583–94 EZ	1963	Daimler Fleetline CRG6	MH Coachworks	H44/31F	1974–80
2596–620	596–620 EZ	1963	Daimler Fleetline CRG6	MH Coachworks	H44/31F	1973–80
2622–26	622–26 EZ	1963	Daimler Fleetline CRG6	MH Coachworks	H44/31F	1977–79
2628	628 EZ	1963	Daimler Fleetline CRG6	MH Coachworks	H44/31F	1977
2630–36	630–36 EZ	1963	Daimler Fleetline CRG6	MH Coachworks	H44/31F	1974–78
2638–40	638–40 EZ	1963	Daimler Fleetline CRG6	MH Coachworks	H44/31F	1974–77
2641	641 FZ	1963	Daimler Fleetline CRG6	MH Coachworks	H44/31F	1973
2642	642 FZ	1964	Daimler Fleetline CRG6	MH Coachworks	H44/31F	1977
2643–45	643–45 FZ	1963	Daimler Fleetline CRG6	MH Coachworks	H44/31F	1973/74
2647–50	647–50 FZ	1963	Daimler Fleetline CRG6	MH Coachworks	H44/31F	1974–77

Fleet Nr	Reg Nr	Built	Chassis Type	Body Type	Seats	Wdn
2652/3	652/3 FZ	1964	Daimler Fleetline CRG6	MH Coachworks	H44/31F	1974–76
2655/6	655/6 FZ	1964	Daimler Fleetline CRG6	MH Coachworks	H44/31F	1974–76
2658	658 FZ	1964	Daimler Fleetline CRG6	MH Coachworks	H44/31F	1976
2661	661 FZ	1964	Daimler Fleetline CRG6	MH Coachworks	H44/31F	1977
2663–65	663–65 FZ	1964	Daimler Fleetline CRG6	MH Coachworks	H44/31F	1973–77
2670	670 FZ	1964	Daimler Fleetline CRG6	MH Coachworks	H44/31F	1981
2672–79	672–79 FZ	1964	Daimler Fleetline CRG6	MH Coachworks	H44/31F	1974–77
2682–85	682–85 FZ	1964	Daimler Fleetline CRG6	MH Coachworks	H44/31F	1974–77
2687–95	687–95 FZ	1964	Daimler Fleetline CRG6	MH Coachworks	H44/31F	1975–80
2698–701	698–701 FZ	1964	Daimler Fleetline CRG6	MH Coachworks	H44/31F	1975–80
2703	703 FZ	1964	Daimler Fleetline CRG6	MH Coachworks	H44/31F	1980
2704/5	1704/5 MZ	1964	Leyland Atlantean PDR1/1	MH Coachworks	H44/31F	1977
2706	1706 MZ	1965	Leyland Atlantean PDR1/1	MH Coachworks	H44/31F	1977
2707–13	707–13 UZ	1967	Daimler Fleetline CRG6	Potter	H44/30F	1974–78
2718–36 [4]	718–36 UZ	1967	Daimler Fleetline CRG6	Potter	H44/30F	1974–81
2737	737 UZ	1968	Daimler Roadliner SRC6	Potter	B44D	1974
2738–42	738–42 UZ	1969	Daimler Roadliner SRC6	Potter	B44D	1976/77
2744	744 UZ	1968	Daimler Roadliner SRC6	Potter	B44D	1977
2745	745 UZ	1969	Daimler Roadliner SRC6	Potter	B44D	1973
2746	746 UZ	1968	Daimler Roadliner SRC6	Potter	B44D	1977
2747–49	747–49 UZ	1969	Daimler Roadliner SRC6	Potter	B44D	1976/77
2750/1	750/1 UZ	1968	Daimler Roadliner SRC6	Potter	B44D	1975–77
2752–54	752–54 UZ	1969	Daimler Roadliner SRC6	Potter	B44D	1975/76
2755	755 UZ	1968	AEC Swift 2P2R	Potter	B46F	1977
2756 [1]	756 UZ	1969	AEC Swift 2P2R	Potter	B46F	1979
2757–63	757–63 UZ	1969	AEC Swift 2P2R	Potter	B46F	1974–79
2764	764 UZ	1968	AEC Swift 2P2R	Potter	B46F	1979
2765/6	765/6 UZ	1969	AEC Swift 2P2R	Potter	B46F	1977/78
2767	767 UZ	1968	AEC Swift 2P2R	Potter	B46F	1978
2768–72	768–72 UZ	1969	AEC Swift 2P2R	Potter	B46F	1977–79
2773 [2]	AOI 773	1969	Daimler Fleetline SRG6LX	Alexander (B)	B43D	1977
2775/6 [2]	AOI 775/6	1970	Daimler Fleetline SRG6LX	Alexander (B)	B43D	1976–80
2777 [2]	AOI 777	1969	Daimler Fleetline SRG6LX	Alexander (B)	B43D	1976
2778/9 [2]	AOI 778/9	1970	Daimler Fleetline SRG6LX	Alexander (B)	B43D	1977–80
2780 [2]	AOI 780	1969	Daimler Fleetline SRG6LX	Alexander (B)	B43D	1981
2781–83 [2]	AOI 781–83	1970	Daimler Fleetline SRG6LX	Alexander (B)	B43D	1977–79
2784	AOI 784	1970	Daimler Fleetline SRG6LX	Alexander (B)	B43D	1974
2785–92 [2]	AOI 785–92	1970	Daimler Fleetline SRG6LX	Alexander (B)	B43D	1976–82
2794–800 [2]	AOI 794–800	1970	Daimler Fleetline SRG6LX	Alexander (B)	B43D	1976–81
2801	AOI 801	1970	Daimler Fleetline SRG6LX	Alexander (B)	B43D	1976
2803	AOI 803	1971	Daimler Fleetline CRG6LX–33	Alexander (B)	H46/31D	1988
2804–09	AOI 804–09	1970	Daimler Fleetline CRG6LX–33	Alexander (B)	H46/31D	1974–80
2811–13	AOI 811–13	1970	Daimler Fleetline CRG6LX–33	Alexander (B)	H46/31D	1976–77
2815–19	AOI 815–19	1970	Daimler Fleetline CRG6LX–33	Alexander (B)	H46/31D	1976–83

Fleet Nr	Reg Nr	Built	Chassis Type	Body Type	Seats	Wdn
2821–26	AOI 821–26	1970	Daimler Fleetline CRG6LX–33	Alexander (B)	H46/31D	1974–83
2830–33	AOI 830–33	1970	Daimler Fleetline CRG6LX–33	Alexander (B)	H46/31D	1974–88
2835	AOI 835	1970	Daimler Fleetline CRG6LX–33	Alexander (B)	H46/31D	1985
2836	AOI 836	1971	Daimler Fleetline CRG6LX–33	Alexander (B)	H46/31D	1977
2837–40	AOI 837–40	1970	Daimler Fleetline CRG6LX–33	Alexander (B)	H46/31D	1976–88
2842–52	AOI 842–52	1970	Daimler Fleetline CRG6LX–33	Alexander (B)	H46/31D	1981–88
2853/4	EOI 4853/4	1972	Daimler Fleetline CRG6LX–33	Alexander (B)	H46/31D	1974–88
2855	EOI 4855	1973	Daimler Fleetline CRG6LX–33	Alexander (B)	H46/31D	1987
2856	EOI 4856	1972	Daimler Fleetline CRG6LX–33	Alexander (B)	H46/31D	1986
2857 [3]	EOI 4857	1973	Daimler Fleetline CRG6LX–33	Alexander (B)	H46/31D	1974
2858	EOI 4858	1972	Daimler Fleetline CRG6LX–33	Alexander (B)	H46/31D	–
2859–61	EOI 4859–61	1973	Daimler Fleetline CRG6LX–33	Alexander (B)	H46/31D	1976–88
2862	EOI 4862	1972	Daimler Fleetline CRG6LX–33	Alexander (B)	H46/31D	–
2864	EOI 4864	1973	Daimler Fleetline CRG6LX–33	Alexander (B)	H46/31D	1976
2866/7	EOI 4866/7	1973	Daimler Fleetline CRG6LX–33	Alexander (B)	H46/31D	1977–88
2868/9	EOI 4868/9	1972	Daimler Fleetline CRG6LX–33	Alexander (B)	H46/31D	1977–88

Notes

1. No 2756 was re–seated to B32F in 1975 but the PSV authorities would not authorise its use as a standee bus and it was returned to its original seating layout.
2. Nos 2773/5–83/5–92/4–800 were re–seated to B31D in 1975/76.
3. No 2857 was loaned to Ulsterbus Ltd. from 8/5/76 to 25/6/76 in exchange for Leyland Atlantean/ Alexander No 947 (COI 947).
4. No 2733 was loaned to Ulsterbus Ltd from 3/11/81 to 31/3/82. It was returned after suffering accident damage and was promptly withdrawn.

Ex-BCT vehicles withdrawn at date of takeover

Fleet Nr	Reg Nr	Wdn	Disposal	Fleet Nr	Reg Nr	Wdn	Disposal
338	MZ 7436	1970	spares/scrap	445	OZ 6699	1972	spares/scrap
339	MZ 7437	1970	spares/scrap	560	560 EZ	1971m	rebodied
345	MZ 7443	1973m	spares/scrap	595	595 EZ	1972m	rebodied
353	OZ 6607	1972	spares/scrap	627	627 EZ	1972m	rebodied
367	OZ 6621	1973	spares/scrap	637	637 EZ	1971m	rebodied
370	OZ 6624	1971m	spares/scrap	651	651 FZ	1972m	rebodied
371	OZ 6625	1971m	spares/scrap	666	666 FZ	1971m	rebodied
395	OZ 6649	1972	spares/scrap	669	669 FZ	1971m	rebodied
398	OZ 6652	1972	spares/scrap	681	681 FZ	1971m	rebodied
399	OZ 6653	1972	spares/scrap	716	716 UZ	1972m	rebodied
401	OZ 6655	1972	spares/scrap	774	AOI 774	1972m	rebodied
402	OZ 6656	1972a	spares/scrap	810	AOI 810	1973m	rebodied
430	OZ 6684	1973	spares/scrap	827	AOI 827	1972m	rebodied

Withdrawal dates of inherited vehicles (in numerical order)

Fleet No	Regist No	Withdrawn	Fleet No	Regist No	Withdrawn	Fleet No	Regist No	Withdrawn	Fleet No	Regist No	Withdrawn
2306	MZ 7404	1975	2397	OZ 6651	1974	2567	567 EZ	1979m	2613	613 EZ	1976m
2307	MZ 7405	1974m	2408	OZ 6662	1973	2568	568 EZ	1978m	2614	614 EZ	1973m
2309	MZ 7407	1975	2409	OZ 6663	1975	2569	569 EZ	1977m	2615	615 EZ	1979m
2310	MZ 7408	1975	2411	OZ 6665	1973m	2570	570 EZ	1975m	2616	616 EZ	1979m
2311	MZ 7409	1975	2412	OZ 6666	1973	2571	571 EZ	1980	2617	617 EZ	1979m
2322	MZ 7420	1975	2413	OZ 6667	1973	2572	572 EZ	1979m	2618	618 EZ	1975m
2323	MZ 7421	1975	2415	OZ 6669	1973	2573	573 EZ	1980	2619	619 EZ	1977m
2326	MZ 7424	1975	2418	OZ 6672	1973	2574	574 EZ	1977m	2620	620 EZ	1980m
2327	MZ 7425	1975	2419	OZ 6673	1973	2575	575 EZ	1973m	2622	622 EZ	1977m
2328	MZ 7426	1975	2420	OZ 6674	1974m	2576	576 EZ	1980m	2623	623 EZ	1977m
2329	MZ 7427	1974m	2421	OZ 6675	1975	2577	577 EZ	1977m	2624	624 EZ	1977m
2330	MZ 7428	1975	2422	OZ 6676	1974	2578	578 EZ	1980	2625	625 EZ	1978m
2332	MZ 7430	1974m	2423	OZ 6677	1973	2579	579 EZ	1980m	2626	626 EZ	1978m
2333	MZ 7431	1975	2424	OZ 6678	1975	2580	580 EZ	1979a	2628	628 EZ	1977m
2334	MZ 7432	1975	2425	OZ 6679	1973	2581	581 EZ	1979	2630	630 EZ	1974m
2335	MZ 7433	1975	2426	OZ 6680	1973	2583	583 EZ	1977m	2631	631 EZ	1976m
2336	MZ 7434	1975	2427	OZ 6681	1975	2584	584 EZ	1980	2632	632 EZ	1976m
2337	MZ 7435	1974m	2428	OZ 6682	1975	2585	585 EZ	1979	2633	633 EZ	1977m
2341	MZ 7439	1974m	2431	OZ 6685	1973	2586	586 EZ	1979	2634	634 EZ	1978m
2343	MZ 7441	1975	2432	OZ 6686	1975p	2587	587 EZ	1980	2635	635 EZ	1974m
2344	MZ 7442	1975	2434	OZ 6688	1975	2588	588 EZ	1974m	2636	636 EZ	1976m
2346	MZ 7444	1975p	2435	OZ 6689	1975	2589	589 EZ	1980	2638	638 EZ	1977m
2347	MZ 7445	1975	2436	OZ 6690	1975	2590	590 EZ	1980	2639	639 EZ	1977m
2348	MZ 7446	1975	2437	OZ 6691	1975	2591	591 EZ	1977m	2640	640 EZ	1974m
2350	OZ 6604	1973	2439	OZ 6693	1973	2592	592 EZ	1980	2641	641 FZ	1973m
2351	OZ 6605	1974	2440	OZ 6694	1975	2593	593 EZ	1980	2642	642 FZ	1977m
2352	OZ 6606	1973m	2442	OZ 6696	1974	2594	594 EZ	1976m	2643	643 FZ	1974m
2355	OZ 6609	1974	2443	OZ 6697	1975a	2596	596 EZ	1980	2644	644 FZ	1973m
2364	OZ 6618	1973m	2444	OZ 6698	1973	2597	597 EZ	1979	2645	645 FZ	1974m
2366	OZ 6620	1975	2446	OZ 6700	1975p	2598	598 EZ	1980	2647	647 FZ	1977m
2367	OZ 6621	1973	2447	OZ 6701	1975a	2599	599 EZ	1974m	2648	648 FZ	1977m
2372	OZ 6626	1975	2448	OZ 6702	1974m	2600	600 EZ	1981	2649	649 FZ	1974m
2376	OZ 6630	1973m	2551	5540 XI	1975s	2601	601 EZ	1979	2650	650 FZ	1977m
2377	OZ 6631	1974m	2553	553 EZ	1976m	2602	602 EZ	1974m	2652	652 FZ	1974m
2379	OZ 6633	1975	2554	554 EZ	1977m	2603	603 EZ	1979m	2653	653 FZ	1976m
2380	OZ 6634	1973m	2555	555 EZ	1977m	2604	604 EZ	1974m	2655	655 FZ	1974m
2381	OZ 6635	1973	2556	556 EZ	1976m	2605	605 EZ	1977m	2656	656 FZ	1976m
2386	OZ 6640	1973	2557	557 EZ	1977m	2606	606 EZ	1977m	2658	658 FZ	1976m
2389	OZ 6643	1975	2558	558 EZ	1977m	2607	607 EZ	1978m	2661	661 FZ	1977m
2390	OZ 6644	1973m	2562	562 EZ	1980m	2608	608 EZ	1975m	2663	663 FZ	1973m
2391	OZ 6645	1975	2563	563 EZ	1977m	2609	609 EZ	1978m	2664	664 FZ	1973m
2392	OZ 6646	1974m	2564	564 EZ	1978m	2610	610 EZ	1978m	2665	665 FZ	1977m
2393	OZ 6647	1973m	2565	565 EZ	1977m	2611	611 EZ	1977m	2670	670 FZ	1981
2394	OZ 6648	1973	2566	566 EZ	1978	2612	612 EZ	1977m	2672	672 FZ	1977m

Fleet No	Regist No	With-drawn	Fleet No	Regist No	With-drawn	Fleet No	Regist No	With-drawn	Fleet No	Regist No	With-drawn
2673	673 FZ	1974m	2727	727 UZ	1977ub	2772	772 UZ	1977m	2822	AOI 822	1974m
2674	674 FZ	1977m	2728	728 UZ	1977ub	2773	AOI 773	1977m	2823	AOI 823	1974m
2675	675 FZ	1977m	2729	729 UZ	1977ub	2775	AOI 775	1980m	2824	AOI 824	1975m
2676	676 FZ	1976m	2730	730 UZ	1977ub	2776	AOI 776	1976m	2825	AOI 825	1983dt
2677	677 FZ	1977m	2731	731 UZ	1976m	2777	AOI 777	1976m	2826	AOI 826	1979m
2678	678 FZ	1977m	2732	732 UZ	1977m	2778	AOI 778	1980m	2829	AOI 829	1974m
2679	679 FZ	1976m	2733	733 UZ	1982a	2779	AOI 779	1977m	2830	AOI 830	1988
2682	682 FZ	1977m	2734	734 UZ	1976m	2780	AOI 780	1981m	2831	AOI 831	1974m
2683	683 FZ	1976m	2735	735 UZ	1979m	2781	AOI 781	1978m	2832	AOI 832	1988
2684	684 FZ	1974m	2736	736 UZ	1974m	2782	AOI 782	1977m	2833	AOI 833	1979m
2685	685 FZ	1977m	2737	737 UZ	1974	2783	AOI 783	1979a	2835	AOI 835	1985
2687	687 FZ	1976m	2738	738 UZ	1976	2784	AOI 784	1974m	2836	AOI 836	1977m
2688	688 FZ	1976m	2739	739 UZ	1977	2785	AOI 785	1982	2837	AOI 837	1976m
2689	689 FZ	1978m	2740	740 UZ	1976m	2786	AOI 786	1982	2838	AOI 838	1981m
2690	690 FZ	1980	2741	741 UZ	1977	2787	AOI 787	1980m	2839	AOI 839	1988
2691	691 FZ	1976m	2742	742 UZ	1977	2788	AOI 788	1978m	2840	AOI 840	1977m
2692	692 FZ	1976m	2744	744 UZ	1977	2789	AOI 789	1980m	2842	AOI 842	1981
2693	693 FZ	1975m	2745	745 UZ	1973m	2790	AOI 790	1980m	2843	AOI 843	1981m
2694	694 FZ	1977m	2746	746 UZ	1977	2791	AOI 791	1976m	2844	AOI 844	1988
2695	695 FZ	1980a	2747	747 UZ	1976	2792	AOI 792	1978m	2845	AOI 845	1988
2698	698 FZ	1977m	2748	748 UZ	1977m	2794	AOI 794	1979m	2846	AOI 846	1988a
2699	699 FZ	1980m	2749	749 UZ	1977m	2795	AOI 795	1976m	2847	AOI 847	1988
2700	700 FZ	1975m	2750	750 UZ	1977	2796	AOI 796	1980m	2848	AOI 848	1983
2701	701 FZ	1977m	2751	751 UZ	1975	2797	AOI 797	1978m	2849	AOI 849	1983dt
2703	703 FZ	1980m	2752	752 UZ	1976	2798	AOI 798	1979m	2850	AOI 850	1988
2704	1704 MZ	1977ub	2753	753 UZ	1975	2799	AOI 799	1977m	2851	AOI 851	1988a
2705	1705 MZ	1977ub	2754	754 UZ	1976	2800	AOI 800	1981m	2852	AOI 852	1987
2706	1706 MZ	1977ub	2755	755 UZ	1977m	2801	AOI 801	1976m	2853	EOI 4853	1974m
2707	707 UZ	1977ub	2756	756 UZ	1979	2803	AOI 803	1988	2854	EOI 4854	1988
2708	708 UZ	1974m	2757	757 UZ	1978m	2804	AOI 804	1980m	2855	EOI 4855	1987m
2709	709 UZ	1977ub	2758	758 UZ	1979	2805	AOI 805	1977m	2856	EOI 4856	1986
2710	710 UZ	1976m	2759	759 UZ	1974m	2806	AOI 806	1977m	2857	EOI 4857	1974m
2711	711 UZ	1977m	2760	760 UZ	1979	2807	AOI 807	1976m	2858	EOI 4858	
2712	712 UZ	1978ub	2761	761 UZ	1978	2808	AOI 808	1977m	2859	EOI 4859	1984m
2713	713 UZ	1977a	2762	762 UZ	1978	2809	AOI 809	1974m	2860	EOI 4860	1976m
2718	718 UZ	1978ub	2763	763 UZ	1979	2811	AOI 811	1977m	2861	EOI 4861	1988
2719	719 UZ	1978ub	2764	764 UZ	1979	2812	AOI 812	1977m	2862	EOI 4862	
2720	720 UZ	1977m	2765	765 UZ	1977m	2813	AOI 813	1976m	2864	EOI 4864	1976m
2721	721 UZ	1977m	2766	766 UZ	1978	2815	AOI 815	1980m	2866	EOI 4866	1988
2722	722 UZ	1978ub	2767	767 UZ	1978	2816	AOI 816	1977m	2867	EOI 4867	1977m
2723	723 UZ	1978ub	2768	768 UZ	1979	2817	AOI 817	1977m	2868	EOI 4868	1977m
2724	724 UZ	1976m	2769	769 UZ	1978	2818	AOI 818	1976m	2869	EOI 4869	1988
2725	725 UZ	1977ub	2770	770 UZ	1977m	2819	AOI 819	1983			
2726	726 UZ	1977ub	2771	771 UZ	1978	2821	AOI 821	1980m			

Vehicles built new for Citybus 1973–1988

Fleet Nr	Reg Nr	Built	Chassis Type	Body Type	Seats	Wdn
2863 [3,4]	EOI 4863	1973	Daimler Fleetline CRG6–33	Alexander (B)	H46/31D	1973
2865 [4]	EOI 4865	1973	Daimler Fleetline CRG6–33	Alexander (B)	H46/31D	–
2870–72 [2,4]	EOI 4870–72	1973	Daimler Fleetline CRG6–33	Alexander (B)	H46/31D	1976–86
2873–912 [1]	JOI 2873–912	1975–76	Leyland Atlantean AN68/2R	Alexander (B)	H49/37F	1976–84
2041–80 [9,10]	LOI 2041–80	1976–77	Bristol RELL6G	Alexander (B)	B32D	1977–91
2081–120 [8,11]	MOI 8081–120	1976–77	Bristol RELL6G	Alexander (B)	B32D	1978–91
2136–70 [8,12]	POI 2136–70	1977–78	Bristol RELL6G	Alexander (B)	B32D	1978–92
2211–30 [8,13,14]	ROI 2211–30	1978	Bristol RELL6G	Alexander (B)	B32D	1978–92
2306–20 [15]	TOI 2306–20	1979	Bristol RELL6G	Alexander (B)	B50F	1992–97
2321–60 [16,17,18]	UOI 2321–60	1979–80	Bristol RELL6G	Alexander (B)	B32D	1981–96
2401–30 [19]	VOI 8401–30	1980–81	Bristol RELL6G	Alexander (B)	B32D	1984–96
2461–80 [20]	WOI 8461–80	1981–82	Bristol RELL6G	Alexander (B)	B39F	1983–2000
2481–530 [20]	XOI 2481–530	1982–84	Bristol RELL6G	Alexander (B)	B39F	1984–2004
3002 [5]	WOI 3002	1981	Leyland B21	Alexander (B)	B43F	–
3003	WOI 3003	1981	Leyland B21	Alexander (B)	B53F	–
3004 [6]	WOI 3004	1982	Leyland B21	Alexander (B)	B33F	–
2531–60 [20,21]	AXI 2531–60	1984–86	Bristol RELL6G	Alexander (B)	B39F	1988–2004
2561–80	BXI 2561–80	1983–85	Bristol RELL6G	Alexander (B)	B52F	–
3006	HXI 3006	1985	Leyland Lynx LX5636LXBFR	Alexander (B)	B37F	–
3007–09 [7]	HXI 3007–09	1986	Leyland Lynx LX5636LXBFR	Alexander (B)	B43F	–
3010 [7]	HXI 3010	1986	Leyland Lynx LX563TL11FR	Alexander (B)	B43F	–
2601–10 [22]	LXI 6601–10	1988	Leyland Tiger TRBLXP/2RP	Alexander (B)	B43F	–

Notes:–

1. No 2911 was loaned to Ulsterbus Ltd from 25/6/76 to 1/9/76 in exchange for Leyland Atlantean/Alexander No 947 (COI 947).
2. No 2872 was loaned to Ulsterbus Ltd from 16/11/81 to 30/3/82.
3. No 2863 was rebodied with new Alexander (Belfast) H46/31D body in 1974 after its original body was destroyed in 1973.
4. Nos 2863/5/70–2 were reseated to H46/30D in 4/78 to allow fitting of new fare collection equipment.
5. No 3002 was reseated to B42F in 2/90.
6. No 3004 was reseated to B42F in 2/90 and again to B46F later in the same year.
7. Nos 3007–10 were reseated to B38F in 6/87 and were used on the NIR Rail–link service from 6/87 to 9/91 (3007/8/10) or 6/87 to 12/91 (3009).
8. Nos 2111/9/63, 2214 were rebodied with new Alexander (Belfast) B32D bodies in 1979 after their original bodies were maliciously destroyed in 1978.
9. Nos 2045/59/62 were reseated to B35D in 1982 and were further reseated to B43D in 1989. Nos 2043/4/6/52/8/60/6/7/75 were reseated to B40D in 1989 and Nos 2044/6/52/8/60/7/75 were further reseated to B43D later in 1989.
10. Nos 2046/7/54–6 were used on the *Citylink* service from 6/76 to 11/76 (2054–6) or from 6/76 to 1/77 (2046/7). Nos 2044–8 were used on the *Citylink* service from 7/78 to 2/80.

11. Nos 2086, 2103/12 were reseated to B35D in 1982 and Nos 2103/12 were further reseated to B43D in 1989. Nos 2087/97 were reseated to B40D in 1989 and then further reseated to B43D later in 1989.
12. Nos 2137/8/41/3–5/8/51/3/8 were reseated to B35D in 1982 and 2144/5/8/51/3 were further reseated to B43D in 1989. Nos 2142/7/9/54–6/9–61/3/9 were reseated to B40D in 1989 and Nos 2142/9/54–6/9–61/3/9 were further reseated to B43D later in 1989.
13. Nos 2211–3/5/6 were used on the *Citylink* service from 2/78 to 3/78 (2211/2/3/6) and from 3/78 to 3/78 (2215).
14. Nos 2219/21/3/4 were reseated to B35D in 1982 and Nos 2219/23 were further reseated to B43D in 1989. Nos 2214/6 were reseated to B40D in 1989 and were further reseated to B43D later in 1989.
15. Nos 2306–20 were reseated to B52F in 1982 and Nos 2306–15 were further reseated to B51F in 1990.
16. Nos 2326/8/34–6/8/40/3/4/7 were reseated to B35D in 1982 and Nos 2326/8/34–6/8/40/4/7 were further reseated to B43D in 1989. Nos 2324/37/45 were reseated to B43D in 1989. Nos 2321–3/7/9–33/48/50–6/8–60 were reseated to B40D in 1989 and were further reseated to B43D later in 1989.
17. Nos 2357–60 were used on the NIR *Rail–link* service from 8/83 to 6/87 (2357/8), 8/83 to 11/87 (2359) and 8/83 to 12/88 (2360).
18. No 2338 was converted to B43F (with centre door sealed) in 1996.
19. Nos 2401/2/5–7/12/3/5 were reseated to B35D in 1982 and Nos 2402/5/6/13/25 were further reseated to B43D in 1989. Nos 2403/4/8–11/4–8/20/1/3/4/6/8/9 were reseated to B40D in 1989 and were further reseated to B43D later in 1989.
20. Nos 2462/3/5–74/7–86/8–500/2/3/5–17/9–54/6–9 were reseated to B45F in 1989. No 2476 was reseated to B45F in 1992.
21. Nos 2531/41/60 were loaned to Ulsterbus Ltd from 4/85 to 6/86 (2531), 8/85 to 4/87 (2560) and 3/86 to 9/87 (2541). 2560 was further loaned to Ulsterbus Ltd from 2/88 until maliciously destroyed in 8/89.
22. Nos 2601–10 were reseated to B42F in 1989/90.

Buses destroyed in civil disturbances and rebodied by W Alexander (Belfast)

Daimler Fleetlines

Fleet Nr	Destroyed	Rebuilt	Body Type	Wdn	Fleet Nr	Destroyed	Rebuilt	Body Type	Wdn
2560	10/1971	11/1973	H44/31F	1975m	2716	6/1972	2/1974	H44/31F	1981ub
2595	8/1972	10/1973	H44/31F	1977m	2774	2/1972	11/1974	B32D	1977m
2627	2/1972	1/1974	H44/31F	1977m	2810	3/1973	3/1974	H46/31D	1979m
2637	10/1971	12/1973	H44/31F	1977m	2827	6/1972	6/1973	H46/31D	1979m
2651	2/1972	1/1974	H44/31F	1977m	2829	11/1974	4/1976	H49/37F	1979m
2666	10/1971	12/1973	H44/31F	1977m	2857	1/1974	4/1976	H49/37F	–
2669	10/1971	9/1973	H44/31F	1977m	2863	7/1973	5/1974	H46/31D	–
2681	10/1971	10/1973	H44/31F	1977m					

Bristol RELL6G

Fleet Nr	Destroyed	Rebuilt	Body Type	Wdn	Fleet Nr	Destroyed	Rebuilt	Body Type	Wdn
2111	4/1978	9/1979	B32D	1980m	2163	4/1978	7/1979	B32D	–
2119	5/1978	9/1979	B32D	1983m	2214	4/1978	9/1979	B32D	–

Withdrawal dates for vehicles built new for Citybus 1974–1988

Fleet No	Regist No	Withdrawn	Fleet No	Regist No	Withdrawn	Fleet No	Regist No	Withdrawn	Fleet No	Regist No	Withdrawn
2041	LOI 2041	1986m	2096	MOI 8096	1979m	2211	ROI 2211	1981m	2871	EOI 4871	1976m
2042	LOI 2042	1980m	2098	MOI 8098	1979m	2212	ROI 2212	1988m	2872	EOI 4872	1986a
2047	LOI 2047	1984m	2099	MOI 8099	1985m	2213	ROI 2213	1979m	2873	JOI 2873	1983
2048	LOI 2048	1980m	2100	MOI 8100	1986m	2214	ROI 2214	1978m	2874	JOI 2874	1979m
2049	LOI 2049	1977m	2101	MOI 8101	1987m	2215	ROI 2215	1979m	2875	JOI 2875	1981m
2050	LOI 2050	1984m	2102	MOI 8102	1983m	2217	ROI 2217	1979m	2876	JOI 2876	1980m
2051	LOI 2051	1984m	2104	MOI 8104	1982m	2218	ROI 2218	1981m	2877	JOI 2877	1984
2053	LOI 2053	1984m	2105	MOI 8105	1980m	2220	ROI 2220	1980m	2878	JOI 2878	1980m
2054	LOI 2054	1987m	2106	MOI 8106	1980m	2221	ROI 2221	1987m	2879	JOI 2879	1983
2055	LOI 2055	1988m	2107	MOI 8107	1987m	2222	ROI 2222	1988m	2880	JOI 2880	1980m
2056	LOI 2056	1984m	2108	MOI 8108	1978m	2224	ROI 2224	1986m	2881	JOI 2881	1983s
2057	LOI 2057	1983m	2109	MOI 8109	1984m	2225	ROI 2225	1978m	2882	JOI 2882	1978m
2061	LOI 2061	1983m	2110	MOI 8110	1979m	2226	ROI 2226	1979m	2883	JOI 2883	1984s
2063	LOI 2063	1981m	2111	MOI 8111	1978m	2227	ROI 2227	1987m	2884	JOI 2884	1980m
2064	LOI 2064	1981m	2113	MOI 8113	1984m	2228	ROI 2228	1979m	2885	JOI 2885	1978m
2065	LOI 2065	1985m	2114	MOI 8114	1980m	2229	ROI 2229	1981m	2886	JOI 2886	1979m
2068	LOI 2068	1982m	2115	MOI 8115	1980m	2230	ROI 2230	1979m	2887	JOI 2887	1983
2069	LOI 2069	1984m	2116	MOI 8116	1981m	2312	TOI 2312	1987m	2888	JOI 2888	1980m
2070	LOI 2070	1984m	2117	MOI 8117	1984m	2325	UOI 2325	1987m	2889	JOI 2889	1980m
2071	LOI 2071	1984m	2118	MOI 8118	1979m	2339	UOI 2339	1984m	2890	JOI 2890	1976m
2072	LOI 2072	1981m	2119	MOI 8119	1978m	2341	UOI 2341	1987m	2891	JOI 2891	1983
2073	LOI 2073	1988m	2120	MOI 8120	1988m	2342	UOI 2342	1987m	2892	JOI 2892	1982m
2074	LOI 2074	1981m	2136	POI 2136	1983m	2343	UOI 2343	1987m	2893	JOI 2893	1986u
2076	LOI 2076	1980m	2137	POI 2137	1988m	2346	UOI 2346	1986m	2894	JOI 2894	1983
2077	LOI 2077	1977m	2138	POI 2138	1983m	2349	UOI 2349	1981a	2895	JOI 2895	1984
2078	LOI 2078	1984m	2139	POI 2139	1988m	2357	UOI 2357	1988m	2896	JOI 2896	1984
2079	LOI 2079	1980m	2140	POI 2140	1986m	2401	VOI 8401	1987m	2897	JOI 2897	1980m
2080	LOI 2080	1987m	2141	POI 2141	1987m	2407	VOI 8407	1986m	2898	JOI 2898	1984s
2081	MOI 8081	1983m	2143	POI 2143	1984m	2419	VOI 8419	1987m	2899	JOI 2899	1982m
2082	MOI 8082	1985m	2146	POI 2146	1982m	2422	VOI 8422	1987m	2900	JOI 2900	1978m
2083	MOI 8083	1987m	2150	POI 2150	1987m	2427	VOI 8427	1984m	2901	JOI 2901	1978m
2084	MOI 8084	1980m	2152	POI 2152	1981m	2430	VOI 8430	1986m	2902	JOI 2902	1980m
2085	MOI 8085	1987m	2157	POI 2157	1986m	2461	WOI 8461	1988m	2903	JOI 2903	1980m
2086	MOI 8086	1985m	2158	POI 2158	1987m	2464	WOI 8464	1988m	2904	JOI 2904	1984
2088	MOI 8088	1980m	2162	POI 2162	1988m	2475	WOI 8475	1983m	2905	JOI 2905	1984
2089	MOI 8089	1988m	2163	POI 2163	1978m	2487	XOI 2487	1988m	2906	JOI 2906	1983
2090	MOI 8090	1987m	2164	POI 2164	1987m	2501	XOI 2501	1984m	2907	JOI 2907	1984s
2091	MOI 8091	1979m	2165	POI 2165	1979m	2504	XOI 2504	1987m	2908	JOI 2908	1976m
2092	MOI 8092	1981m	2166	POI 2166	1979m	2518	XOI 2518	1988m	2909	JOI 2909	1976m
2093	MOI 8093	1980m	2167	POI 2167	1984m	2555	AXI 2555	1988m	2910	JOI 2910	1978m
2094	MOI 8094	1980m	2168	POI 2168	1979m	2863	EOI 4863	1973m	2911	JOI 2911	1981m
2095	MOI 8095	1985m	2170	POI 2170	1979m	2870	EOI 4870	1976m	2912	JOI 2912	1978m

Pre-owned vehicles acquired by Citybus 1974–1988

Fleet No	Reg No	New	Into Service	Chassis Type	Body Type	Seats	Wdn
Ex-Coastal Bus Services, Portrush (via Ulsterbus Ltd), in April 1974							
1298	KVT 175E	1967	–	Daimler SRC6	Marshall	B50F	n.o.
1299	7901 YZ	1967	1974	Daimler SRC6	Marshall	B49F	1976
Ex-Ulsterbus Ltd, Belfast, in March–October 1974							
1001	SWS 1	1959	1974	Leyland PSUC1/3	Weymann	B43F	1975
1003	SWS 3	1959	1974	Leyland PSUC1/3	Weymann	B43F	1977
1004	SWS 4	1959	–	Leyland PSUC1/3	Weymann	B43F	n.o.
1008	SWS 8	1959	1974	Leyland PSUC1/3	Weymann	B43F	1977
1010	SWS 10	1959	1974	Leyland PSUC1/3	Weymann	B43F	1974
1012	SWS 12	1959	1974	Leyland PSUC1/3	Weymann	B43F	1976
1015	SWS 15	1959	1974	Leyland PSUC1/3	Weymann	B43F	1975
1018	SWS 18	1959	–	Leyland PSUC1/3	Weymann	B43F	n.o.
1024	SWS 24	1959	1974	Leyland PSUC1/3	Weymann	B43F	1977
1025	SWS 25	1959	1974	Leyland PSUC1/3	Weymann	B43F	1974
1027	SWS 27	1959	1974	Leyland PSUC1/3	Weymann	B43F	1977
1029	SWS 29	1959	1974	Leyland PSUC1/3	Weymann	B43F	1976
1030	SWS 30	1959	1974	Leyland PSUC1/3	Weymann	B43F	1975
1032	SWS 32	1959	1974	Leyland PSUC1/3	Weymann	B43F	1976
1033	SWS 33	1959	1974	Leyland PSUC1/3	Weymann	B43F	1975
1034	SWS 34	1959	–	Leyland PSUC1/3	Weymann	B43F	n.o.
1037	SWS 37	1959	1974	Leyland PSUC1/3	Weymann	B43F	1975
1038	SWS 38	1959	1974	Leyland PSUC1/3	Weymann	B43F	1976
1040	SWS 40	1959	–	Leyland PSUC1/3	Weymann	B43F	n.o.
1041	SWS 41	1959	1974	Leyland PSUC1/3	Weymann	B43F	1975
1042	SWS 42	1959	1974	Leyland PSUC1/3	Weymann	B43F	1977
1043	SWS 43	1959	–	Leyland PSUC1/3	Weymann	B43F	n.o.
1046	SWS 46	1959	1974	Leyland PSUC1/3	Weymann	B43F	1977
1048	SWS 48	1959	–	Leyland PSUC1/3	Weymann	B43F	n.o.
Ex-Ulsterbus Ltd, Belfast, in January–June 1975							
987/9	1987/9 OI	1959	1975	Leyland PD3/5	UTA	FH39/28F	1975
1017	SWS 17	1959	1975	Leyland PSUC1/3	Weymann	B43F	1976
1019	SWS 19	1959	1975	Leyland PSUC1/3	Weymann	B43F	1975
1026	SWS 26	1959	–	Leyland PSUC1/3	Weymann	B43F	n.o.
1031	SWS 31	1959	1975	Leyland PSUC1/3	Weymann	B43F	1977
1035	SWS 35	1959	1975	Leyland PSUC1/3	Weymann	B43F	1977
1044	SWS 44	1959	1975	Leyland PSUC1/3	Weymann	B43F	1976
1045	SWS 45	1959	1975	Leyland PSUC1/3	Weymann	B43F	1977
1050	SWS 50	1959	1975	Leyland PSUC1/3	Weymann	B43F	1975

Fleet No	Reg No	New	Into Service	Chassis Type	Body Type	Seats	Wdn
Ex-Ulsterbus Ltd, Belfast, in September 1975							
1300	CIA 3000	1966	–	AEC Swift MP2R	Marshall	B48F	n.o.
Ex-Ulsterbus Ltd, Belfast, in January 1977							
1005	SWS 5	1959	–	Leyland PSUC1/3	Weymann	B43F	1977
1011	SWS 11	1959	1977	Leyland PSUC1/3	Weymann	B43F	1977
1023	SWS 23	1959	–	Leyland PSUC1/3	Weymann	B43F	n.o.
1028	SWS 28	1959	1977	Leyland PSUC1/3	Weymann	B43F	1977
1039	SWS 39	1959	–	Leyland PSUC1/3	Weymann	B43F	n.o.
Ex-London Transport in February 1977							
2531	VLW 351G	1968	1977	AEC Merlin 4P2R	MCW	B49F	1978
2532–5	WMT xxxG	1969	1977	AEC Merlin 4P2R	MCW	B49F	1981/82
2536–50	AML xxxH	1969	1977	AEC Merlin 4P2R	MCW	B49F	1979–82
Ex-London Transport in March 1977							
2523–30	VLW xxxG	1968	1977	AEC Merlin 4P2R	MCW	B32D	1977–81
Ex-London Transport in July 1977 (for spare parts)							
–	VLW 26G	1968	–	AEC Merlin 3P2R	MCW	B46D	n.o.
–	VLW 165G	1968	–	AEC Merlin 3P2R	MCW	B50F	n.o.
–	VLW 386G	1968	–	AEC Merlin 4P2R	MCW	B50F	n.o.
Ex-Potteries Motor Traction, Stoke on Trent, in April–August 1977							
2920–35	BEH xxxH	1970	1977	Daimler SRG6LX-33	Alexander	B40D	1978–83
Ex-London Transport in September 1977							
2498	VLW 451G	1968	1977	AEC Merlin 4P2R	MCW	B25D	1981
2499	VLW 510G	1969	1977	AEC Merlin 4P2R	MCW	B25D	1980
2500–5	AML xxxH	1969	1977	AEC Merlin 4P2R	MCW	B25D	1978–81
Ex-London Transport in November 1977							
2489	VLW 454G	1968	–	AEC Merlin 4P2R	MCW	B25D	n.o.
2490–4	VLW xxxG	1969	–	AEC Merlin 4P2R	MCW	B25D	n.o.
2495	VLW 546G	1969	1978	AEC Merlin 4P2R	MCW	B25D	1979
2496	AML 548H	1969	–	AEC Merlin 4P2R	MCW	B25D	n.o.
2497	AML 576H	1969	1978	AEC Merlin 4P2R	MCW	B25D	1981
Ex-London Transport in February–December 1978							
1	EGN 187J	1970	–	AEC Swift 4MP2R/1	Marshall	B32D	n.o.
2	EGN 198J	1970	1978	AEC Swift 4MP2R/1	Marshall	B32D	1980
3–4	EGN 205/6J	1970	1978	AEC Swift 4MP2R/1	Marshall	B32D	1979–80
5	EGN 209J	1971	1978	AEC Swift 4MP2R/1	Marshall	B32D	1980
6	EGN 373G	1970	1978	AEC Swift 4MP2R/1	Park Royal	B32D	1980
7/8	EGN 374/80J	1970	–	AEC Swift 4MP2R/1	Park Royal	B32D	n.o.

Fleet No	Reg No	New	Into Service	Chassis Type	Body Type	Seats	Wdn
9	EGN 590J	1971	–	AEC Swift 4MP2R/1	Metro Cammell	B32D	n.o.
10	EGN 596J	1971	–	AEC Swift 4MP2R/2	Metro Cammell	B32D	n.o.
11/2	EGN 558/9J	1971	1978	AEC Swift 4MP2R/1	Metro Cammell	B32D	1978/79
13	EGN 560J	1971	–	AEC Swift 4MP2R/1	Metro Cammell	B32D	n.o.
14–16	EGN 561–3J	1971	1978	AEC Swift 4MP2R/1	Metro Cammell	B32D	1978–80
17	EGN 579J	1971	1978	AEC Swift 4MP2R/2	Metro Cammell	B32D	1980
18	EGN 608J	1971	–	AEC Swift 4MP2R/2	Metro Cammell	B32D	n.o.
19	EGN 539J	1971	1978	AEC Swift 4MP2R/1	Metro Cammell	B32D	1979
20	EGN 546J	1971	1979	AEC Swift 4MP2R/1	Metro Cammell	B32D	1980
21/2	EGN 557/77J	1971	1978	AEC Swift 4MP2R/1	Metro Cammell	B32D	1980
23/4	EGN 591/2J	1971	1979	AEC Swift 4MP2R/2	Metro Cammell	B32D	1980
25	EGN 594J	1971	–	AEC Swift 4MP2R/2	Metro Cammell	B32D	n.o.
26	EGN 660J	1971	–	AEC Swift 4MP2R/3	Metro Cammell	B32D	n.o.
27	EGN 664J	1971	1978	AEC Swift 4MP2R/3	Metro Cammell	B32D	1979
28	EGN 350J	1970	1978	AEC Swift 4MP2R/1	Park Royal	B32D	1980
29	EGN 565J	1971	1979	AEC Swift 4MP2R/2	Metro Cammell	B32D	1980
30	EGN 578J	1971	1979	AEC Swift 4MP2R/1	Metro Cammell	B32D	1979
31	EGN 607J	1971	1978	AEC Swift 4MP2R/2	Metro Cammell	B32D	1979
32–37	EGN xxxJ	1971	1978	AEC Swift 4MP2R/3	Metro Cammell	B32D	1979–80
38	EGN 204J	1970	1978	AEC Swift 4MP2R/1	Marshall	B32D	1980
39	EGN 540J	1971	1978	AEC Swift 4MP2R/1	Metro Cammell	B32D	1980
40	EGN 568J	1971	1979	AEC Swift 4MP2R/1	Metro Cammell	B32D	1980
41/2	EGN 582/9J	1971	1978	AEC Swift 4MP2R/1	Metro Cammell	B32D	1980
43	EGN 606J	1971	1978	AEC Swift 4MP2R/2	Metro Cammell	B32D	1980
44	EGN 616J	1971	1978	AEC Swift 4MP2R/3	Metro Cammell	B32D	1980
45	EGN 688J	1971	1979	AEC Swift 4MP2R/3	Metro Cammell	B32D	1980
46/7	EGN 692/4J	1971	1979	AEC Swift 4MP2R/4	Metro Cammell	B32D	1979/80
48/9	EGN 580/3J	1971	1979	AEC Swift 4MP2R/1	Metro Cammell	B32D	1980
50	EGN 611J	1971	1978	AEC Swift 4MP2R/3	Metro Cammell	B32D	1980
51	EGN 654J	1971	1979	AEC Swift 4MP2R/3	Metro Cammell	B32D	1979
52/3	EGN 685/7J	1971	1978	AEC Swift 4MP2R/3	Metro Cammell	B32D	1979/80
54	JGF 704K	1971	1979	AEC Swift 4MP2R/4	Metro Cammell	B32D	1980
55/6	EGN 677/91J	1971	1979	AEC Swift 4MP2R/3	Metro Cammell	B32D	1979
57	JGF 722K	1971	1979	AEC Swift 4MP2R/4	Metro Cammell	B32D	1980
58	JGF 781K	1971	1979	AEC Swift 4MP2R/5	Metro Cammell	B32D	1980
71	AML 64H	1970	1979	AEC Swift 4MP2R	Park Royal	B42F	1980
72	EGN 434J	1971	–	AEC Swift 4MP2R/2	Park Royal	B42F	n.o.
73	EGN 439J	1971	1979	AEC Swift 4MP2R/2	Park Royal	B42F	1980
74/5	EGN 442/3J	1971	1979	AEC Swift 4MP2R/3	Park Royal	B42F	1980
76	EGN 447J	1971	–	AEC Swift 4MP2R/3	Park Royal	B42F	n.o.
77	EGN 429J	1971	1978	AEC Swift 4MP2R/1	Park Royal	B42F	1980
78	EGN 445J	1971	1978	AEC Swift 4MP2R/3	Park Royal	B40D	1980
79	EGN 446J	1971	–	AEC Swift 4MP2R/3	Park Royal	B42F	n.o.
80	AML 84H	1970	1970	AEC Swift 4MP2R	Park Royal	B42F	1980

Fleet No	Reg No	New	Into Service	Chassis Type	Body Type	Seats	Wdn
Ex-Northern General, Gateshead, in March 1978							
2936–48	LCN xxxK	1972	1978	Daimler SRG6LX-36	Willowbrook	B44D	1978–81
2949/50	NCN 64/6L	1972	1978	Daimler SRG6LX-36	Willowbrook	B44D	1979–81
Ex-Ulsterbus Ltd, Belfast, in April 1978							
2500/1	AML 572/86H	1969	1978	AEC Merlin 4P2R	MCW	B25D	1978
2503	AML 604H	1969	1978	AEC Merlin 4P2R	MCW	B25D	1979
2505	AML 613H	1969	1978	AEC Merlin 4P2R	MCW	B25D	1978
Ex-Ulsterbus Ltd, Belfast, in September 1978							
2502	AML 603H	1969	1978	AEC Merlin 4P2R	MCW	B25D	1981
Ex-London Transport in March–May 1979							
59/60	JGF 795/6K	1971	–	AEC Swift 4MP2R/5	Metro Cammell	B32D	n.o.
61–63	AML xxH	1970	–	AEC Swift 4MP2R	Park Royal	B42F	n.o.
64/5	EGN 430/2J	1971	–	AEC Swift 4MP2R/2	Park Royal	B42F	n.o.
66	EGN 384J	1970	–	AEC Swift 4MP2R/1	Park Royal	B42F	n.o.
67	EGN 414J	1971	–	AEC Swift 4MP2R/1	Park Royal	B42F	n.o.
68	EGN 448J	1971	1979	AEC Swift 4MP2R/3	Park Royal	B42F	1980
69/70	AML 73/81H	1970	–	AEC Swift 4MP2R	Park Royal	B42F	n.o.
Ex-London Country Bus Services, Reigate, in April–August 1979							
621	SMM 82F	1968	1979	AEC Merlin 3P2R	MCW	B45D	1982
622	SMM 91F	1968	–	AEC Merlin 3P2R	MCW	B45D	n.o.
623	VLW 95G	1968	1979	AEC Merlin 3P2R	MCW	B45D	1982
624–34	VLW xxxG	1968	1979	AEC Merlin 4P2R	MCW	B33D	1980–82
635	SMM 81F	1968	1979	AEC Merlin 3P2R	MCW	B45D	1981
636	VLW 93G	1968	–	AEC Merlin 3P2R	MCW	B45D	n.o.
637	VLW 104G	1968	1980	AEC Merlin 3P2R	MCW	B45D	1982
638	VLW 272G	1968	–	AEC Merlin 4P2R	MCW	B33D	n.o.
639	VLW 275G	1968	1979	AEC Merlin 4P2R	MCW	B33D	1979
640	VLW 300G	1968	1980	AEC Merlin 4P2R	MCW	B33D	1982
641	VLW 402G	1968	1979	AEC Merlin 4P2R	MCW	B33D	1980
642	VLW 407G	1968	–	AEC Merlin 4P2R	MCW	B33D	n.o.
643/4	VLW 408/10G	1968	1980	AEC Merlin 4P2R	MCW	B33D	1981
645	VLW 102G	1968	1979	AEC Merlin 3P2R	MCW	B45D	1981
646	VLW 103G	1968	1980	AEC Merlin 3P2R	MCW	B45D	1981
647	VLW 110G	1968	1979	AEC Merlin 3P2R	MCW	B45D	1981
648	VLW 111G	1968	1980	AEC Merlin 3P2R	MCW	B45D	1982
649–52	VLW xxxG	1968	1980	AEC Merlin 4P2R	MCW	B33D	1981
653	VLW 400G	1968	1979	AEC Merlin 4P2R	MCW	B33D	1981
654	VLW 401G	1968	1980	AEC Merlin 4P2R	MCW	B33D	1982
655/6	VLW 429/30G	1968	1979	AEC Merlin 4P2R	MCW	B33D	1980/81
657	VLW 437G	1968	1980	AEC Merlin 4P2R	MCW	B33D	1981

Fleet No	Reg No	New	Into Service	Chassis Type	Body Type	Seats	Wdn
Ex-Mid-Warwickshire Motors, Balsall Common, in May 1979							
2551–4	AML xxxH	1969	1979	AEC Merlin 4P2R	MCW	B49F	1980/81
Ex-London Transport in August 1979 (for spare parts)							
–	VLW 77G	1968	–	AEC Merlin 3P2R	MCW	B32D	n.o.
–	JGF 813K	1972	–	AEC Swift 4MP2R	Metro Cammell	B33D	n.o.
Ex-Ulsterbus Ltd, Belfast, in December 1979							
15	EGN 562J	1971	1979	AEC Swift 4MP2R/1	Metro Cammell	B32D	1980
Ex-Ulsterbus Ltd, Belfast, in February/March 1980							
4	EGN 206J	1970	1980	AEC Swift 4MP2R/1	Marshall	B32D	1980
13	EGN 560J	1971	1980	AEC Swift 4MP2R/1	Metro Cammell	B32D	1980
17	EGN 579J	1971	1980	AEC Swift 4MP2R/2	Metro Cammell	B32D	1980
18	EGN 608J	1971	1980	AEC Swift 4MP2R/2	Metro Cammell	B32D	1980
25	EGN 594J	1971	1980	AEC Swift 4MP2R/2	Metro Cammell	B32D	1980
1218/59	1218/59 TZ	1967	1980	Bedford VAM 14	Duple	DP45F	1980
2490	VLW 460G	1969	1980	AEC Merlin 4P2R	MCW	B25D	1980
2497	AML 576H	1969	1980	AEC Merlin 4P2R	MCW	B25D	1981
2511–3	VLW xxxG	1968	1980	AEC Merlin 4P2R	MCW	B50F	1981
2517/8	VLW 364/87G	1968	1980	AEC Merlin 4P2R	MCW	B50F	1981
2522	VLW 366G	1968	1980	AEC Merlin 4P2R	MCW	B50F	1981
Ex-Ulsterbus Ltd, Belfast, in May 1980							
2508	VLW 370G	1968	1980	AEC Merlin 4P2R	MCW	B50F	1980
Ex-London Country Bus Services, Reigate, in May 1980							
658/9	SMM 87/9F	1968	–	AEC Merlin 3P2R	MCW	B45D	n.o.
660	VLW 96G	1968	–	AEC Merlin 3P2R	MCW	B45D	n.o.
661	VLW 109G	1969	–	AEC Merlin 3P2R	MCW	B45D	n.o.
662	VLW 270G	1970	–	AEC Merlin 4P2R	MCW	B33D	n.o.
663–9	VLW xxxG	1969	–	AEC Merlin 4P2R	MCW	B33D	n.o.
Ex-Crosville Motor Services, Chester, in March–November 1980							
700–3	OFM xxE	1967	1980	Bristol RELL6G	ECW	B53F	1981–87
704/5	SFM 21/2F	1967	1980	Bristol RELL6G	ECW	B53F	1985–89
706	UFM 44F	1968	1980	Bristol RELL6G	ECW	B53F	1989
707–9	OFM xxE	1967	1980	Bristol RELL6G	ECW	B53F	1984–86
710	OFM 15E	1967	1981	Bristol RELL6G	ECW	B53F	1984
711/2	SFM 17/8F	1967	1981	Bristol RELL6G	ECW	B53F	1982–84
713	SFM 19F	1967	1980	Bristol RELL6G	ECW	B53F	1982
714	SFM 20F	1967	1981	Bristol RELL6G	ECW	B53F	1986
715	UFM 42F	1968	1980	Bristol RELL6G	ECW	B53F	1982

Fleet No	Reg No	New	Into Service	Chassis Type	Body Type	Seats	Wdn
Ex-United Automobile Services, Darlington, in June–December 1980							
716/7	THN 888/92F	1968	1980	Bristol RELL6G	ECW	B53F	1982/83
718	WHN 397G	1969	1980	Bristol RELL6G	ECW	B53F	1982
719–22	THN xxxF	1968	1980	Bristol RELL6G	ECW	B53F	1981–83
723	THN 895F	1968	–	Bristol RELL6G	ECW	B53F	n.o.
724	THN 896F	1968	1980	Bristol RELL6G	ECW	B53F	1981
725/6	THN 887/90F	1968	1981	Bristol RELL6G	ECW	B53F	1981–88
727	YHN 802H	1969	1981	Bristol RELL6G	ECW	B53F	1983
728	WHN 399G	1969	1981	Bristol RELL6G	ECW	B53F	1981
729/30	YHN 804/6H	1969	1981	Bristol RELL6G	ECW	B53F	1984
Ex-Ulsterbus Ltd, Belfast, in September 1980 (for conversion to towing vehicle)							
480	7480 CZ	1962	n.o.	Leyland PSUC1/12	UTA	DP41F	n.o.
Ex-Ulsterbus Ltd, Belfast in January/February 1981 (for conversion to towing vehicles)							
428	7428 CZ	1962	n.o.	Leyland PSUC1/12	UTA	DP41F	n.o.
458	7458 CZ	1962	n.o.	Leyland PSUC1/12	UTA	DP41F	n.o.
Ex-United Automobile Services, Darlington, in January/February 1981							
731	WHN 398G	1969	1981	Bristol RELL6G	ECW	B53F	1983
732	WHN 401G	1969	1981	Bristol RELL6G	ECW	B53F	1981
Ex-Crosville Motor Services, Chester, in March 1981							
734	UFM 46F	1968	1981	Bristol RELL6G	ECW	B53F	1989
Ex-West Yorkshire Road Car, Harrogate, in July 1981							
735	BWU 552H	1969	1981	Bristol RELL6G	ECW	B53F	1988
736	BWW 152H	1969	1982	Bristol RELL6G	ECW	B53F	1983
737/8	BYG 542/3H	1969	1981	Bristol RELL6G	ECW	B53F	1987
Ex-Crosville Motor Services, Chester, in July 1981							
739	AFM 117G	1969	1981	Bristol RELL6G	ECW	B53F	1983
740–3	UFM xxF	1968	1981	Bristol RELL6G	ECW	B53F	1982–89
744	AFM 119G	1969	1981	Bristol RELL6G	ECW	B53F	1985
Ex-Ulsterbus Ltd, Belfast, in April 1982 (for conversion to driver training vehicle)							
2712	712 UZ	1967	n.o.	Daimler CRG6	Potter	H44/30F	n.o.
Ex-West Riding Automobile, Wakefield, in May 1983							
745–8	WHL xxxJ	1971	1983	Bristol RELL6G	ECW	B53F	1984–88
749	AHL 232K	1971	1983	Bristol RELL6G	ECW	B53F	1987
750	AHL 233K	1971	1984	Bristol RELL6G	ECW	B53F	1984
751	CHL 637K	1972	1984	Bristol RELL6G	ECW	B53F	1984

Fleet No	Reg No	New	Into Service	Chassis Type	Body Type	Seats	Wdn
Ex-West Yorkshire Road Car, Harrogate, in May–July 1983							
757	LWR 798K	1971	1984	Bristol RELL6G	ECW	B53F	1986
758	TWX 195L	1972	1984	Bristol RELL6G	ECW	B53F	1990
759	RWT 764K	1972	1984	Bristol RELL6G	ECW	B53F	1984
760	VWT 678L	1973	1984	Bristol RELL6G	ECW	B53F	1985
761/2	NWU 322/3M	1973	1984	Bristol RELL6G	ECW	B53F	1990
763	TWX 199L	1972	1984	Bristol RELL6G	ECW	B53F	1990
764	VWT 681L	1973	1984	Bristol RELL6G	ECW	B53F	1984
Ex-United Automobile Services, Darlington, in October 1984							
768	JHN 342K	1971	1984	Bristol RELL6G	ECW	B50F	1985
769	JHN 354K	1972	1984	Bristol RELL6G	ECW	B50F	1987
770/1	JHN 348/9K	1971	1984	Bristol RELL6G	ECW	B50F	1985
772/3	NHN 766/9K	1972	1985	Bristol RELL6G	ECW	B50F	1988–90
774	PHN 175L	1972	1985	Bristol RELL6G	ECW	B50F	1985
Ex-East Midland Motor Services, Chesterfield, in October 1984							
775/6	GVO 550/6K	1972	1985	Bristol RELL6G	ECW	B49F	1985–90
Ex-West Yorkshire Road Car, Harrogate, in November 1984							
777	UWX 372L	1973	1985	Bristol RELL6G	ECW	B53F	1988
Ex-United Automobile Services, Darlington, in December 1984							
778	JHN 347K	1971	1985	Bristol RELL6G	ECW	B50F	1987
779	JHN 358K	1972	1985	Bristol RELL6G	ECW	B50F	1985
780/1	NHN 765/8K	1972	1985	Bristol RELL6G	ECW	B50F	1988
784	OHN 463L	1972	1986	Bristol RELL6G	ECW	B50F	1987
785	PHN 172L	1972	1987	Bristol RELL6G	ECW	B50F	1987
Ex-Ulsterbus Ltd, Belfast, in December 1984 (for conversion to towing vehicles)							
1717	HOI 1717	1974	n.o.	Bedford YRQ	Alexander (B)	B45F	n.o.
1763	HOI 1763	1974	n.o.	Bedford YRQ	Alexander (B)	B45F	n.o.
1784	HOI 1784	1974	n.o.	Bedford YRQ	Alexander (B)	B45F	n.o.
Ex-Eastern National Omnibus, Chelmsford, in February 1985							
790	KVX 570J	1970	1987	Bristol RELL6G	ECW	B53F	1988
791–3	MHK xxxJ	1971	1987	Bristol RELL6G	ECW	B53F	1988/89
794	RPU 884K	1972	1987	Bristol RELL6G	ECW	B53F	1987
Ex-United Automobile Services, Darlington, in November 1985							
702(2)	OHN 462L	1972	1987	Bristol RELL6G	ECW	B50F	1989
797	JHN 356K	1972	1986	Bristol RELL6G	ECW	B50F	1987
798	PHN 170L	1972	1986	Bristol RELL6G	ECW	B50F	1987
799/800	PHN 171/4L	1972	1987	Bristol RELL6G	ECW	B50F	1987

Fleet No	Reg No	New	Into Service	Chassis Type	Body Type	Seats	Wdn
Ex-Eastern National Omnibus, Chelmsford, in April 1986							
704(2)	OHK 226K	1971	1987	Bristol RELL6G	ECW	B53F	1989
707(2)	PEV 501K	1971	1987	Bristol RELL6G	ECW	B53F	1988
709/10(2)	PEV 502/3K	1971	1987	Bristol RELL6G	ECW	B53F	1988–90
711(2)	RPU 882K	1972	1987	Bristol RELL6G	ECW	B53F	1989
712/3(2)	SVW 273/5K	1972	1987	Bristol RELL6G	ECW	B53F	1988/89
714/5(2)	WNO 538/41L	1972	1987	Bristol RELL6G	ECW	B53F	1987/88
717/8(2)	WNO 542/3L	1972	1987	Bristol RELL6G	ECW	B53F	1989
Ex-Ulsterbus Ltd, Belfast, in April 1987							
561/2	XOI 561/2	1981	1987	Leyland PSU3E/4R	Plaxton	C49F	1992
Ex-Crosville Motor Services, Chester, in June 1987							
703/8(2)	HFM 198/9J	1970	1987	Bristol RELL6G	ECW	B48D	1989
Ex-Wilts & Dorset Bus Co, Poole, in June 1987							
714(3)	TRU 948J	1971	1988	Bristol RELL6G	ECW	DP50F	1989
Ex-United Counties Omnibus Co, Northampton, in June 1987							
716(2)	RBD 330G	1968	1987	Bristol RELL6G	ECW	B53F	1989
724(2)	RBD 319G	1968	1988	Bristol RELL6G	ECW	B53F	1990
Ex-Crosville Motor Services, Chester, in July 1987							
726–8(2)	HFM xxxJ	1970	1988	Bristol RELL6G	ECW	B48D	1989/90
729(2)	XFM 75G	1968	1988	Bristol RESL6G	ECW	B46F	1988
Ex-Cumberland Motor Services, Whitehaven, in August 1987							
730(2)	MHW 282L	1973	1988	Bristol RELL6L	ECW	B44D	1988
731(2)	OHU 36M	1973	1988	Bristol RELL6L	ECW	B44D	1990
732(2)	HHW 920L	1972	1988	Bristol RELL6L	ECW	B44D	1990
739/41(2)	OHU 34/8M	1973	1988	Bristol RELL6L	ECW	B44D	1989/90
742–4(2)	MHW xxxL	1973	1988	Bristol RELL6L	ECW	B44D	1988/89
746(2)	OHU 37M	1973	1988	Bristol RELL6L	ECW	B44D	1990
Ex-Ribble Motor Services, Preston, in August 1987							
733	OCK 342K	1971	1988	Bristol RESL6L	ECW	B47F	1989
736(2)	OCK 347K	1971	1989	Bristol RESL6L	ECW	B47F	1989
738(2)	OCK 353K	1972	1988	Bristol RESL6L	ECW	B47F	1990
Ex-Ulsterbus Ltd, Belfast, in September–December 1987							
2232	ROI 2232	1978	1987	Bristol RELL6G	Alexander (B)	B52F	1993
2276	TOI 2276	1979	1987	Bristol RELL6G	Alexander (B)	B52F	1992
2287/9	TOI 2287/9	1979	1987	Bristol RELL6G	Alexander (B)	B52F	1991/92
2301	TOI 2301	1979	1987	Bristol RELL6G	Alexander (B)	B52F	1996
2363	UOI 2363	1980	1987	Bristol RELL6G	Alexander (B)	B52F	1995
2442/53	WOI 2442/53	1981	1987	Bristol RELL6G	Alexander (B)	B52F	1996/97
2591	BXI 2591	1983	1987	Bristol RELL6G	Alexander (B)	B52F	1995

Fleet No	Reg No	New	Into Service	Chassis Type	Body Type	Seats	Wdn
Ex-Crosville Wales, Llandudno, in September 1987							
747(2)	EFM 178H	1970	1988	Bristol RELL6G	ECW	B53F	1989
748/9(2)	EFM 181/2H	1970	1989	Bristol RELL6G	ECW	B53F	1990
750(2)	HFM 208J	1970	1988	Bristol RELL6G	ECW	B53F	1989
Ex-United Automobile Services, Darlington, in March 1988							
751–3(2)	JHN xxxK	1972	1989	Bristol RESL6G	ECW	B47F	1989/90
754(2)	JHN 563K	1972	–	Bristol RESL6G	ECW	B47F	n.o.
756(2)	HHN 723K	1971	–	Bristol RESL6G	ECW	B47F	n.o.
757(2)	JHN 557K	1972	–	Bristol RESL6G	ECW	B47F	n.o.
759(2)	OHN 468L	1972	–	Bristol RESL6G	ECW	B47F	n.o.
760(2)	JHN 564K	1972	–	Bristol RESL6G	ECW	B47F	n.o.
Ex-Ribble Motor Services, Preston, in April 1988							
764(2)	NCK 338J	1971	1988	Bristol RESL6L	ECW	B47F	1990
765(2)	OCK 355K	1972	1988	Bristol RESL6L	ECW	B47F	1990
766(2)	OCK 350K	1971	1988	Bristol RESL6L	ECW	B47F	1990
767(2)	OCK 359K	1972	–	Bristol RESL6L	ECW	B47F	n.o.
768(2)	NCK 340J	1971	1988	Bristol RESL6L	ECW	B47F	1990
Ex-Yelloway Motor Services, Rochdale, in May 1988							
769(2)	LTG 35L	1972	1989	Bristol RESL6L	ECW	B44F	1989
770(2)	JEH 187K	1971	1989	Bristol RESL6L	ECW	B44F	1989
771(2)	NHB 188M	1973	1989	Bristol RESL6G	ECW	B47F	1989
773(2)	LTG 41L	1972	1989	Bristol RESL6L	ECW	B44F	1989
Ex-Ribble Motor Services, Preston, in July 1988							
774(2)	OCK 368K	1972	–	Bristol RESL6L	ECW	B47F	n.o.
776(2)	NCK 337J	1971	–	Bristol RESL6L	ECW	B47F	n.o.
Ex-Cambus, Cambridge, in September 1988							
777(2)	YNG 725J	1970	1989	Bristol RELL6G	ECW	B53F	1990
778(2)	WNG 864H	1970	–	Bristol RELL6G	ECW	DP50F	n.o.
779(2)	XAH 873H	1970	–	Bristol RELL6G	ECW	DP50F	n.o.
Ex-West Sussex County Council in November 1988							
780/2(2)	LRC 343/5K	1972	–	Bristol RELL6G	ECW	B49F	n.o.

Fleet No	Reg No	New	Into Service	Chassis Type	Body Type	Seats	Wdn
Ex-Ulsterbus Ltd, Belfast, in January–November 1988							
721	NCK 331J	1971	1988	Bristol RESL6L	ECW	B47F	1989
722	NCK 335J	1971	1988	Bristol RESL6L	ECW	B47F	1989
723	NCK 334J	1971	–	Bristol RESL6L	ECW	B47F	n.o.
789	MHK 914J	1971	1988	Bristol RELL6G	ECW	B53F	1989
2173/9	POI 2173/9	1977	1988	Bristol RELL6G	Alexander (B)	B52F	1991
2241/2	ROI 2241/2	1978	1988	Bristol RELL6G	Alexander (B)	B52F	1991/92
2246/7	ROI 2246/7	1978	1988	Bristol RELL6G	Alexander (B)	B52F	1992
2261	ROI 2261	1979	1988	Bristol RELL6G	Alexander (B)	B52F	1992
2288	TOI 2288	1979	1988	Bristol RELL6G	Alexander (B)	B52F	1992
2296/7/9	TOI 2296/7/9	1979	1988	Bristol RELL6G	Alexander (B)	B52F	1989–92
2361	UOI 2361	1979	1988	Bristol RELL6G	Alexander (B)	B52F	1995
2362	UOI 2362	1980	1988	Bristol RELL6G	Alexander (B)	B52F	1996
2433	WOI 2433	1980	1988	Bristol RELL6G	Alexander (B)	B52F	1997

Note:-

Nos 2173/9, 2232/41/2/6/61/76/87-9/97/9, 2301/61-3, 2433/42/53 were reseated to B51F in 1990.

Fleet No	Reg No	New	Into Service	Chassis Type	Body Type	Seats	Wdn
Ex-Kettlewell, Retford, in November 1988							
785(2)	GHY 132K	1972	–	Bristol RELH6G	ECW	DP49F	n.o.
Ex-Cumberland Motor Services, Whitehaven, in December 1988							
786(2)	VOD 102K	1971	–	Bristol RELL6G	ECW	B53F	n.o.
Ex-North Western Road Car, Bootle, in January/February 1989							
781	OCK 345K	1971	–	Bristol RESL6L	ECW	B47F	n.o.
783/4	OCK 356/61K	1971	–	Bristol RESL6L	ECW	B47F	n.o.
787	OCK 344K	1971	1989	Bristol RESL6L	ECW	B47F	1989
788	OCK 358K	1972	1989	Bristol RESL6L	ECW	B47F	1990
790/1	OCK 369/70K	1972	–	Bristol RESL6L	ECW	B47F	n.o.
792	OCK 363K	1972	–	Bristol RESL6L	ECW	B47F	n.o.

Withdrawal dates of pre-owned vehicles

Fleet No	Regist No	Withdrawn	Fleet No	Regist No	Withdrawn	Fleet No	Regist No	Withdrawn	Fleet No	Regist No	Withdrawn
1	EGN 187J	n.o.	9	EGN 590J	n.o.	16	EGN 563J	1978m	23	EGN 591J	1980
2	EGN 198J	1980m	10	EGN 596J	n.o.	17	EGN 579J	1978ub	24	EGN 592J	1980m
3	EGN 205J	1979m	11	EGN 558J	1979m	17	EGN 579J	1980	25	EGN 594J	1978ub
4	EGN 206J	1978ub	12	EGN 559J	1978ub	18	EGN 608J	n.o.*	25	EGN 594J	1980m
4	EGN 206J	1980	13	EGN 560J	n.o.*	18	EGN 608J	1980	26	EGN 660J	n.o.
5	EGN 209J	1980	13	EGN 560J	1980	19	EGN 539J	1979m	27	EGN 664J	1979m
6	EGN 373J	1980	14	EGN 561J	1978ub	20	EGN 546J	1980m	28	EGN 350J	1980
7	EGN 374J	n.o.	15	EGN 562J	1978ub	21	EGN 557J	1980	29	EGN 565J	1980m
8	EGN 380J	n.o.	15	EGN 562J	1980	22	EGN 577J	1980	30	EGN 578J	1979m

Fleet No	Regist No	Withdrawn	Fleet No	Regist No	Withdrawn	Fleet No	Regist No	Withdrawn	Fleet No	Regist No	Withdrawn
31	EGN 607J	1979m	624	VLW 277G	1980m	679	AML 652H	1982	729	YHN 804H	1984
32	EGN 609J	1980	625	VLW 279G	1980m	680	AML 659H	1982	729(2)	XFM 75G	1988m
33	EGN 652J	1979m	626	VLW 289G	1982	681	AML 661H	1982	730	YHN 806H	1984
34	EGN 662J	1979	627	VLW 296G	1981	700	OFM 9E	1984m	730(2)	MHW 282L	1988m
35	EGN 669J	1980	628	VLW 409G	1981	701	OFM 11E	1988m	731	WHN 398G	1983m
36	EGN 680J	1980m	629	VLW 411G	1981	702	OFM 14E	1981a	731(2)	OHU 36M	1990s
37	EGN 684J	1980	630	VLW 413G	1981	702(2)	OHN 462L	1989m	732	WHN 401G	1981a
38	EGN 204J	1980	631	VLW 431G	1980m	703	OFM 16E	1987m	732(2)	HHW 920L	1990s
39	EGN 540J	1980	632	VLW 433G	1982	703(2)	HFM 198J	1989	733	OCK 342K	1989a
40	EGN 568J	1980	633	VLW 436G	1982	704	SFM 21F	1985m	734	UFM 46F	1989m
41	EGN 582J	1980	634	VLW 438G	1982	704(2)	OHK 226K	1989m	735	BWU 552H	1988a
42	EGN 589J	1980	635	SMM 81F	1981m	705	SFM 22F	1989	736	BWW 152H	1983m
43	EGN 606J	1980	636	VLW 93G	n.o.	706	UFM 44F	1989	736(2)	OCK 347K	1989m
44	EGN 616J	1980	637	VLW 104G	1982	707	OFM 10E	1984m	737	BYG 542H	1987m
45	EGN 688J	1980	638	VLW 272G	n.o.	707(2)	PEV 501K	1988m	738	BYG 543H	1987m
46	EGN 692J	1979a	639	VLW 275G	1979m	708	OFM 12E	1986m	738(2)	OCK 353K	1990s
47	EGN 694J	1980	640	VLW 300G	1982	708(2)	HFM 199J	1989m	739	AFM 117G	1983m
48	EGN 580J	1980	641	VLW 402G	1980	709	OFM 13E	1984m	739(2)	OHU 34M	1989m
49	EGN 583J	1980	642	VLW 407G	n.o.	709(2)	PEV 502K	1990m	740	UFM 43F	1989
50	EGN 611J	1980	643	VLW 408G	1981m	710	OFM 15E	1984m	741	UFM 45F	1982m
51	EGN 654J	1979m	644	VLW 410G	1981	710(2)	PEV 503K	1988	741(2)	OHU 38M	1990s
52	EGN 685J	1980	645	VLW 102G	1981a	711	SFM 17F	1984m	742	UFM 47F	1984m
53	EGN 687J	1979	646	VLW 103G	1981	711(2)	RPU 882K	1989m	742(2)	MHW 284L	1988m
54	JGF 704K	1980	647	VLW 110G	1981	712	SFM 18F	1982m	743	UFM 48F	1984m
55	EGN 677J	1979m	648	VLW 111G	1982	712(2)	SVW 273K	1988m	743(2)	MHW 281L	1989m
56	EGN 691J	1979	649	VLW 273G	1981	713	SFM 19F	1982m	744	AFM 119G	1985m
57	JGF 722K	1980	650	VLW 291G	1981	713(2)	SVW 275K	1989m	744(2)	MHW 283L	1989
58	JGF 781K	1980	651	VLW 292G	1981	714	SFM 20F	1986m	745	WHL 730J	1988m
59	JGF 795K	n.o.	652	VLW 399G	1981m	714(2)	WNO 538L	1987m	746	WHL 731J	1984m
60	JGF 796K	n.o.	653	VLW 400G	1981	714(3)	TRU 948J	1989dt	746(2)	OHU 37M	1990
61	AML 65H	n.o.	654	VLW 401G	1982	715	UFM 42F	1982m	747	WHL 733J	1984m
62	AML 74H	n.o.	655	VLW 429G	1980a	715(2)	WNO 541L	1988m	747(2)	EFM 178H	1989
63	AML 87H	n.o.	656	VLW 430G	1981	716	THN 888F	1983m	748	WHL 734J	1984m
64	EGN 430J	n.o.	657	VLW 437G	1981a	716(2)	RBD 330G	1989m	748(2)	EFM 181H	1990
65	EGN 432J	n.o.	658	SMM 87F	n.o.	717	THN 892F	1982m	749	AHL 232K	1987m
66	EGN 384J	n.o.	659	SMM 89F	n.o.	717(2)	WNO 542L	1989	749(2)	EFM 182H	1990
67	EGN 414J	n.o.	660	VLW 96G	n.o.	718	WHN 397G	1982m	750	AHL 233K	1984m
68	EGN 448J	1980	661	VLW 109G	n.o.	718(2)	WNO 543L	1989	750(2)	HFM 208J	1989m
69	AML 73H	n.o.	662	VLW 270G	n.o.	719	THN 889F	1981m	751	CHL 637K	1984m
70	AML 81H	n.o.	663	VLW 286G	n.o.	720	THN 891F	1981m	751(2)	JHN 566K	1989
71	AML 64H	1980	664	VLW 287G	n.o.	721	THN 893F	1981m	752(2)	JHN 565K	1989m
72	EGN 434J	n.o.	665	VLW 414G	n.o.	721(2)	NCK 331J	1989	753(2)	JHN 561K	1990
73	EGN 439J	1980	666	VLW 421G	n.o.	722	THN 894F	1983m	754(2)	JHN 563K	n.o.
74	EGN 442J	1980m	667	VLW 422G	n.o.	722(2)	NCK 335J	1989	756(2)	HHN 723K	n.o.
75	EGN 443J	1980	668	VLW 423G	n.o.	723	THN 895F	n.o.	757	LWR 798K	1986m
76	EGN 447J	n.o.	669	VLW 425G	n.o.	723(2)	NCK 334J	n.o.	757(2)	JHN 557K	n.o.
77	EGN 429J	1980m	670	AML 576H	1981	724	THN 896F	1981m	758	TWX 195L	1990
78	EGN 445J	1980	671	VLW 451G	1981	724(2)	RBD 319G	1990p	759	RWT 764K	1984m
79	EGN 446J	n.o.	672	AML 603H	1981	725	THN 887F	1988m	759(2)	OHN 468L	n.o.
80	AML 84H	1980m	673	VLW 346G	1982	726	THN 890F	1981m	760	VWT 678L	1985m
561	XOI 561	1992ub	674	VLW 364G	1982m	726(2)	HFM 190J	1989m	760(2)	JHN 564K	n.o.
562	XOI 562	1992ub	675	VLW 222G	1981	727	YHN 802H	1983m	761	NWU 322M	1990
621	SMM 82F	1982	676	WMT 619G	1982	727(2)	HFM 192J	1990	762	NWU 323M	1990
622	SMM 91F	n.o.	677	WMT 620G	1981	728	WHN 399G	1981m	763	TWX 199L	1990
623	VLW 95G	1982	678	AML 625H	1981	728(2)	HFM 196J	1990p	764	VWT 681L	1984m

Fleet No	Regist No	With-drawn	Fleet No	Regist No	With-drawn	Fleet No	Regist No	With-drawn	Fleet No	Regist No	With-drawn
764(2)	NCK 338J	1990	1017	SWS 17	1976	2489	VLW 454G	n.o.	2547	AML 654H	1981a
765(2)	OCK 355K	1990	1018	SWS 18	n.o.	2490	VLW 460G	n.o.*	2548	AML 659H	see 680
766(2)	OCK 350K	1990	1019	SWS 19	1975	2490	VLW 460G	1980m	2549	AML 661H	see 681
767(2)	OCK 359K	n.o.	1023	SWS 23	n.o.	2491	VLW 461G	n.o.*	2550	AML 664H	1981m
768	JHN 342K	1985m	1024	SWS 24	1977	2492	VLW 465G	n.o.*	2551	AML 634H	1981
768(2)	NCK 340J	1990	1025	SWS 25	1974	2493	VLW 518G	n.o.	2552	AML 636H	1980m
769	JHN 354K	1987m	1026	SWS 26	n.o.	2494	VLW 527G	n.o.*	2553	AML 663H	1980m
769(2)	LTG 35L	1989s	1027	SWS 27	1977	2495	VLW 546G	1979m	2554	AML 665H	1981
770	JHN 348K	1985m	1028	SWS 28	1977	2496	AML 548H	n.o.	2591	BXI 2591	1995ub
770(2)	JEH 187K	1989	1029	SWS 29	1976	2497	AML 576H	n.o.*	2920	BEH 140H	1982
771	JHN 349K	1985m	1030	SWS 30	1975	2497	AML 576H	see 670	2921	BEH 142H	1981m
771(2)	NHB 188M	1989s	1031	SWS 31	1977	2498	VLW 451G	see 671	2922	BEH 144H	1982
772	NHN 766K	1990	1032	SWS 32	1976	2499	VLW 510G	1980m	2923	BEH 145H	1982
773	NHN 769K	1988m	1033	SWS 33	1975	2500	AML 572H	1978ub	2924	BEH 146H	1982
773(2)	LTG 41L	1989s	1034	SWS 34	n.o.	2500	AML 572H	1978m	2925	BEH 148H	1979m
774	PHN 175L	1985m	1035	SWS 35	1977	2501	AML 586H	1978ub	2926	BEH 149H	1978m
774(2)	OCK 368K	n.o.	1037	SWS 37	1975	2501	AML 586H	1978m	2927	BEH 150H	1979m
775	GVO 550K	1990s	1038	SWS 38	1976	2502	AML 603H	1978ub	2928	BEH 151H	1977m
776	GVO 556K	1985m	1039	SWS 39	n.o.	2502	AML 603H	see 672	2929	BEH 152H	1982dt
776(2)	NCK 337J	n.o.	1040	SWS 40	n.o.	2503	AML 604H	1978ub	2930	BEH 154H	1980m
777	UWX 372L	1988m	1041	SWS 41	1975	2503	AML 604H	1979m	2931	BEH 155H	1983
777(2)	YNG 725J	1990s	1042	SWS 42	1977	2504	AML 610H	1978m	2932	BEH 157H	1983
778	JHN 347K	1987m	1043	SWS 43	n.o.	2505	AML 613H	1978ub	2933	BEH 158H	1979m
778(2)	WNG 864H	1988dt	1044	SWS 44	1976	2505	AML 613H	1978m	2934	BEH 156H	1978m
779	JHN 358K	1985m	1045	SWS 45	1977	2508	VLW 370G	1980	2935	BEH 160H	1982
779(2)	XAH 873H	1988dt	1046	SWS 46	1977	2511	VLW 346G	see 673	2936	LCN 501K	1979m
780	NHN 765K	1988m	1048	SWS 48	n.o.	2512	VLW 352G	1981	2937	LCN 502K	1981m
780(2)	LRC 343K	n.o.	1050	SWS 50	1975	2513	VLW 353G	1981m	2938	LCN 505K	1981
781	NHN 768K	1988m	1218	1218 TZ	1980m	2517	VLW 364G	see 674	2939	LCN 510K	1978m
782(2)	LRC 345K	n.o.	1259	1259 TZ	1980	2518	VLW 387G	1981m	2940	LCN 511K	1979m
784	OHN 463L	1987m	1298	KVT 175E	n.o.	2522	VLW 366G	1981m	2941	LCN 515K	1979m
785	PHN 172L	1987m	1299	7901 YZ	1976	2523	VLW 207G	1980	2942	LCN 516K	1981m
785(2)	GHY 132K	n.o.	1300	CIA 3000	n.o.	2524	VLW 209G	1977m	2943	LCN 517K	1981
786(2)	VOD 102K	n.o.	2173	POI 2173	1991be	2525	VLW 214G	1977m	2944	LCN 518K	1979m
789	MHK 914J	1989	2179	POI 2179	1991be	2526	VLW 216G	1977m	2945	LCN 519K	1981m
790	KVX 570J	1988m	2232	ROI 2232	1992ub	2527	VLW 220G	1977m	2946	LCN 521K	1979m
791	MHK 912J	1988m	2241	ROI 2241	1991m	2528	VLW 222G	see 675	2947	LCN 522K	1980
792	MHK 915J	1988m	2242	ROI 2242	1992ub	2529	VLW 230G	1981m	2948	LCN 523K	1981
793	MHK 916J	1989m	2246	ROI 2246	1992ub	2530	VLW 232G	1977m	2949	NCN 64L	1979m
794	RPU 884K	1987m	2247	ROI 2247	1989m	2531	VLW 351G	1978	2950	NCN 66L	1981
797	JHN 356K	1987m	2261	ROI 2261	1992m	2532	WMT 616G	1981m			
798	PHN 170L	1987m	2276	ROI 2276	1992ub	2533	WMT 617G	1981			
799	PHN 171L	1987m	2287	ROI 2287	1992ub	2534	WMT 619G	see 676			
800	PHN 174L	1987m	2288	ROI 2288	1992a	2535	WMT 620G	see 677			
987	1987 OI	1975	2289	ROI 2289	1991m	2536	AML 625H	see 678			
989	1989 OI	1975	2296	ROI 2296	1989m	2537	AML 627H	1981m			
1001	SWS 1	1975	2297	ROI 2297	1992ub	2538	AML 632H	1981			
1003	SWS 3	1977a	2299	ROI 2299	1992ub	2539	AML 637H	1982			
1004	SWS 4	n.o.	2301	ROI 2301	1996ub	2540	AML 639H	1981m			
1005	SWS 5	1977	2361	UOI 2361	1995	2541	AML 643H	1981m			
1008	SWS 8	1977	2362	UOI 2362	1996ub	2542	AML 644H	1980			
1010	SWS 10	1974	2363	UOI 2363	1995a	2543	AML 646H	1981m			
1011	SWS 11	1977	2433	WOI 2433	1997ub	2544	AML 647H	1979m			
1012	SWS 12	1976	2442	WOI 2442	1996	2545	AML 652H	see 679			
1015	SWS 15	1975	2453	WOI 2453	1997ub	2546	AML 653H	1982			

Vehicles allocated for driver training

Daimler Fleetline

Fleet No	In	Out	Fleet No	In	Out	Fleet No	In	Out	Fleet No	In	Out
2581	7/79	11/80	2587	1/81	5/83	2825	5/83	4/89	2924	5/81	10/81*
2585	11/80	4/81	2597	7/79	11/80	2849	5/83	1/88a	2929	5/81	10/81*
2586	7/79	2/80m	2712	4/82	5/83p	2863	6/88	4/89*	2929	3/82	8/82*

AEC Swift

Fleet No	In	Out	Fleet No	In	Out	Fleet No	In	Out	Fleet No	In	Out
2755	6/77	8/77*	2766	9/77	10/77*	2766	9/78	6/79	2771	4/78	5/78*
2764	6/77	8/77*	2766	4/78	5/78*	2767	9/77	10/77*			

* after withdrawal date indicates that the vehicle was returned to passenger use.

Vehicles allocated for towing

Leyland Tiger Cub PSUC1/12

Fleet No	In	Out	Fleet No	In	Out	Fleet No	In	Out
428	2/81	12/84	458	3/81	2/85	480	9/80	12/84

Bedford YRQ

Fleet No	In	Out	Fleet No	In	Out	Fleet No	In	Out
1717	12/84	9/94	1763	12/84	12/93	1784	12/84	1/93

Also available from Colourpoint Books

 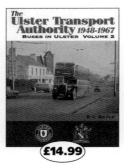 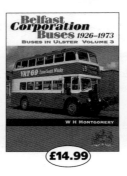 

£11.99 — £14.99 — £14.99 — £15.99

 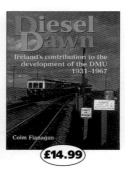 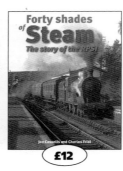 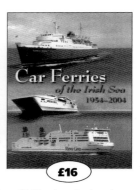

£16 — £14.99 — £12 — £16

All major credit cards accepted. Mail order: UK post free, ROI £1. Overseas: surface £3.50, airmail at cost.

New titles in preparation:
Buses under fire, NI buses during the Troubles — *Autumn 2005*
Buses in Ulster Vol 6 Ulsterbus & Citybus 1988–2002 — *Spring 2006*

Irish Transport Trust
Interested in buses and coaches?

Then why not join the Irish Transport Trust?

We hold monthly meetings/slide shows in Belfast from September to April, as well as the annual Bus & Coach Rally at the end April. Regular trips to places of interest.

More information from

The Honorary Chairman, Irish Transport Trust,
14 Mayfields, LISBURN, BT28 3RP

www.irishtransporttrust.freeserve.co.uk